What's With the

MUTANT

in the
Microscope?

Books by Kevin Johnson

Early Teen Devotionals

Can I Be a Christian Without Being Weird?
Could Someone Wake Me Up Before I Drool on the Desk?
Does Anybody Know What Planet My Parents Are From?
So Who Says I Have to Act My Age?
Was That a Balloon or Did Your Head Just Pop?
Who Should I Listen To?
Why Can't My Life Be a Summer Vacation?
Why Is God Looking for Friends?

Books for Teens

Catch the Wave!
Find Your Fit (with Jane A. G. Kise)
Find Your Fit Discovery Workbook (with Jane A. G. Kise)
Look Who's Toast Now!
What Do Ya Know?
What's With the Dudes at the Door? (with James White)
What's With the Mutant in the Microscope? (with James White)

To find out more about Kevin Johnson's books,
visit his Web site: www.thewave.org

Books by James White

The Forgotten Trinity
Grieving: Our Path Back to Peace
Is the Mormon My Brother?
The King James Only Controversy
Letters to a Mormon Elder
The Roman Catholic Controversy

To find out more about James White's books,
visit his website: www.aomin.org

KEVIN JOHNSON JAMES S. WHITE

What's With the MUTANT in the Microscope?

BETHANY HOUSE PUBLISHERS
MINNEAPOLIS, MINNESOTA 55438

What's With the Mutant in the Microscope?
Copyright © 1999
Kevin Johnson and James R. White

Cover illustration by Scott Angle
Cover by Lookout Design Group, Inc.

Published by Bethany House Publishers
A Ministry of Bethany Fellowship International
11400 Hampshire Avenue South
Minneapolis, Minnesota 55438
www.bethanyhouse.com

Printed in the United States of America by
Bethany Press International, Minneapolis, Minnesota 55438

Library of Congress Cataloging-in-Publication Data

Johnson, Kevin (Kevin Walter)
    What's with the mutant in the microscope? : stuff to know when
science says your uncle is a monkey / by Kevin Johnson & James White.
        p. cm.
Summary: Explains the arguments in the creation versus evolution debate,
answers the claims that humans are the product of chance, and presents a
clear case for the Biblical teachings on creationism.
    ISBN 0-7642-2187-6
1. Creationism. [1. Creationism. 2. Evolution.] I. White, James R.
(James Robert), 1962– II. Title.
BS651 .J59 1999
231.7'652—dc21   99–006883
                                                              CIP

From Kevin:

To my dad,
Roy Johnson,
for teaching me to think hard
about God and goo.

From James:

For my awesome kids,
Josh and Summer,
and all the young Christians who,
like I, want to stand for
God's truth in the classroom.

KEVIN JOHNSON served as senior editor for adult nonfiction at Bethany House Publishers and pastored a cool group of more than four hundred sixth through ninth graders at Elmbrook Church in metro Milwaukee. While his training includes an M.Div. from Fuller Theological Seminary and a B.A. in English and Print Journalism from the University of Wisconsin–River Falls, his current interests include cycling, guitar, and shortwave radio. Kevin and his wife, Lyn, live in Minnesota with their three children—Nate, Karin, and Elise.

JAMES WHITE is director of ministries for Alpha and Omega Ministries, a Christian apologetics organization based in Phoenix, Arizona, and an adjunct professor with Golden Gate Baptist Theological Seminary's Arizona campus. He is also professor of apologetics with Columbia Evangelical Seminary, a critical consultant for the Lockman Foundation on the *New American Standard Bible* update, and an elder in the Phoenix Reformed Baptist Church.

Contents

CHAPTER 1

Your Uncle Was Fuzzy— Or Was He?

"Although atheism might have been *logically* tenable before Darwin, Darwin made it possible to be an intellectually fulfilled atheist."

RICHARD DAWKINS
British Biologist
The Blind Watchmaker (1986)

Josh glanced at the handout his teacher had plopped on his desk, a stack of papers titled "How Life Began." He didn't have to page far before he landed on a chart of a dwarfy ape-like creature evolving step by step into a human.

His gut churned. *I knew this was coming,* he groaned. *I should have faked sick. Stayed away. Hung around home.*

Josh is a Christian. He reads his Bible, wants to follow Christ, and believes what the Bible says. He knows enough to see himself as God's *creation,* so he has big problems with any theory that he's the descendant of some long-lost Uncle Monkey.

He's known for a long time he would run head-on into a battle this year in science class. . . .

The Bible versus science . . .
Creation versus evolution . . .
Ape people or the image of God . . .
God's design or the dumb luck of random mutations . . .
Lightning-ignited seashore ooze or the breath of God in Adam's nostrils.

It's not like he hadn't seen this stuff before, because it was all around him on the walls of his science classroom, in his textbooks, in the offhand comments of his teachers. But reckoning time has come. Josh knows he has a choice to make. And he doesn't get even a minute to think.

"Now, before we begin," Mr. Kregel says with great authority, "I suppose I should ask if anyone has a problem with the issue of evolution."

Snickers from the back of the room. Josh looks around. No raised hands.

"I mean, there are those who, well, for *religious* reasons, do not accept the evidence for evolution."

Josh wants to duck, but he doesn't feel right about letting a point-blank question fly by. Time to do it. Here we go. His hand slowly rises.

Mr. Kregel's brow bunches up like a caterpillar and he says, "Yes, Josh?"

"Well . . ." *Why does the back of my head feel so warm?* Josh feels every eye staring at him, like hot laser beams carving I-D-I-O-T in his skull's backside. "I don't think the evolutionary theory is the only possible explanation," he begins. "Lots of people believe we are the result of a special creation by—"

The teacher waves a hand. "Now, we can't talk about religion in a science class," he says. "But we surely respect those whose religious beliefs require them to believe in the Genesis account of creation." *Yeah, sure. R-E-S-P-E-C-T. So why doesn't Mr. Kregel shut up the snickers in the back of the room?*

"It's not just a religious thing," Josh tries to respond. "I've read works by scientists who have serious questions about the evolutionary theory."

Mr. Kregel smiles knowingly. "Yes, there are what religious folk call 'creation scientists,' but really, Josh, no one in the scientific community takes them seriously. Science makes no statements about religion. Science just deals with facts, and the facts are indisputably clear that evolution is the only *logical* explanation for how life as we know it arose."

With that, Mr. Kregel turns to the board and begins writing. Subject closed. The class moves on, and Josh does his best to cool his head despite the lingering stares of everyone who had just crowned him king of the religious weirdos.

Walking down the hall after school, Josh hears some guys talking about class. "Hey, Josh," one yells. "Come here!"

Josh walks over.

"So what's this you believe about creation? You think God made the earth in six days? That there was an Adam and Eve, and all that stuff? How can anyone believe that anymore? Science is proof. Creation is a myth."

"I don't think science proves *anything* like that," Josh replies. "Lots of people who know the facts don't come to the conclusions you do."

"Yeah, sure. That's why they teach us 'creation science'

in school" comes the mocking reply. "Josh, you have a brain. Admit it! The only reason you don't accept the fact of evolution is that you believe in the Bible. That's all you have to go on."

"I do believe the Bible," Josh says, finally getting a little defensive, "but I don't have to unplug my brain to do it. There are plenty of reasons to think we were created by God and didn't just happen to come into existence."

"Yeah, sure," the crowd chants. "Give us one good reason."

Give Them One Good Reason

What's *your* answer to that invitation?

What "one good reason" could you offer your skeptical friends and teachers to get them to entertain the idea that you and they were made by God? Lots of Christians are in one of three uncomfortable spots:

- Maybe you've been taught that God created the world—and you're sure that's true. But you're not so sure how the scientific data helps or hurts what you believe.
- Maybe you've mastered arguments for six-day creation, flood geology, and a young earth—but your "creation science" gets smirked out of science class. You're not sure how to go mind-to-mind with people who think differently from you.
- Maybe you've slunk through both Sunday school and science class—and you jumble creation and evolution together. You figure they teach pretty much the same thing.

The conflict that Josh experienced is no illusion, no exaggeration, nothing new or unusual from middle school to high school to university and grad school. Creation and evolution can't both be true. In fact, the theories of creation and evolution are like two trains hurtling at high speed from opposite directions down the same how-did-we-get-here? track. They're bound to crash. Check this out:

Creationism says . . .	Evolution says . . .
You are the handiwork of an intelligent being	You are one link in a mindless process
You are the product of divine creation	You are the product of purely natural forces
You were made for a purpose	You are the result of a chance accident
You are a unique creation	You are the descendent of ape-like ancestors

Whether you know a lot or a little about the creation-evolution debate, you might feel unsure about that "one good reason" why you aren't a brain-dead I-D-I-O-T to believe God made the universe.

We're going to assume you accept as "one good reason" the Bible's message that we were made by God. But when you stand up in science class or talk with your friends about creation and evolution, that reason probably won't fly. Pointing to the Bible and saying "I believe in creation because the Bible says so" won't cut it for most people. They choose biology over the Bible, science over Sunday school, goo over God. They've almost for sure been taught that the scientific evidence for evolution is a five-hundred-pound gorilla and that—on the laboratory balance—arguments for creation weigh less than a feather.

Is the Bible all you have to go on?

Or is there another good reason to believe in creation—a reason drawn from the scientific data itself?

The Heart of the Matter and the Heat of the Battle

The most *basic* question about the origin and development of life isn't about *how long*. It's about *who*.

And nature itself supplies that other good reason to believe in creation: design.

The more science uncovers about life, the more it displays inescapable evidence of *design*.

And if there's design, there's an intelligent designer. A worldmaker. A creator of you, me, and the natural world we see. A *who* who made you.

That's the most fundamental claim of creationism.

It's really what the dispute boils down to.

Here's why. If you have proof that what you see in the world is the product of dumb luck, that's all you need to dispense with a designer.

In most people's minds, that's the choice: Could every living thing come to exist on its own through random forces—or does it take a creator to explain what we see?

Problem is, the evolutionary theory we're all taught doesn't even allow that question. Contemporary science claims to offer "no comment" about God's existence, ruling God outside its realm of knowledge. Science says, moreover, that its job is to explain how everything we see in the world came about through *natural* forces, apart from any supernatural invention—or intervention. It's a small step from there to where science fans often wind up: arguing that nothing even exists beyond what's seen, a belief system called "scientific naturalism" or "materialism," completely denying God's existence.

But here's the big point: When evolution becomes an unquestioned *assumption* or *presupposition* guiding all else, its believers are unwilling to face the fact that random forces aren't enough to explain the diversity of life on planet earth.

Nature begs for a better explanation.

So here's what *What's With the Mutant in the Microscope?* is all about: *Demonstrating the truth of creation requires showing how evolutionary theory can't explain what we see—and how the real "Facts of Life" point to a designer.*

Tossed Off the Train of Thought

Wait a minute.

Is proving or disproving one theory or another really that important? If creationism is one train of thought and evolutionary theory is another, can't we weld them together and ride both trains? After all, aren't they actually going in the same direction? Aren't they describing the same thing in different ways? It might feel reasonable, say, to buy one ticket that says that God created the world and another ticket that says evolution is the method God used to develop His creation from *point A* to *point B* to *points C, D*, and *Z*.

That wouldn't be prudent. It might be possible—if you were really big-brained and wearing both superscientist long undies and a super-Christian cape—to swoop between trains. But only *if* they were chugging toward the same destination. Even superheroes can't ride two ideas speeding in opposite directions. Here's the truth: Creationism and evolution are two wildly opposite ways of looking at you and your universe.

In reality, evolutionary theory tosses you and your Creator, God, off its train. Like we just saw, it doesn't *need* God. In fact, because of the rules science sets for itself, it doesn't *allow* God in the picture—not when Charles Darwin thunk up the theory, not now, not ever. Science rejects your understanding of God—in other words, it trash-talks your theology.

The flipside is also true. Good theology refuses to get hitched to science's run-of-the-mill, no-God-needed theory of evolution, and for several reasons. Creationism insists, *ahem*, on God's intimate involvement in planetary development—exactly what science forbids—because it reflects what we see in the Bible of God's care for the world from Creation until the end of time. Creationism also doubts a divine designer would create life using evolution's dumb-luck approach, just like no human engineer would throw a motherboard, memory, and miscellaneous parts into the wind and wait for a computer to whirl into existence. Besides that, creationists say, the Creator of the world would pick a mechanism that works—and we think the *scientific* evidence says evolution doesn't.

Beware of the Borg

Truth is, your skeptical friends aren't the only ones who need reasons to believe. *You* do. Just like Josh, sooner or later you'll stumble into the origins dispute. Since the Bible's basic teaching that God is your creator is denied by evolutionary theory as it is taught in most schools—and since evolution is taken as total fact even in many Christian colleges—you're faced with either "believing the Bible" or "believing the facts."

You've got to beware of the Borg.

Huh?

Let us explain.

In *Star Trek*—not in the old "Beam Me Up, Scotty" version but the later "Next Generation" world of Worf, Troy, Data, and Captain Jean-Luc Picard—there's a race known as the Borg roaming the galaxy gobbling up other peoples. When the Borg encounters a new species, its robot-like members utter two ugly taunts: "Resistance is futile" and "You will be assimilated."

Students who are unprepared to answer the claims of evolution—on evolution's own terms—are foolishly unaware of the Borg-like quality of evolutionary theory. If you're unprepared to disarm the Borg, you'll be assimilated. Swallowed up. Wired for the other side. You'll choose to embrace the "facts," shrinking the Bible to "faith" or "myth" or "mere religion." And you'll live in a haunting reality: If you think God didn't make you, you'll think He doesn't matter.

Firing Blanks

So why is it that creationists get laughed at while evolutionists get white lab coats with pocket protectors and "Dr. So and So" sewn on? Is the evidence so utterly overwhelming that no one who knows squat about science would ever call themselves a creationist?

No way. Christians have been intimidated into thinking they hold the short end of the factual stick. As we'll see throughout *What's With the Mutant in the Microscope?* there is all around us ample evidence of the Creator. It's possible to be *fully* aware of scientific methodology and fact and still reject evolution as an unworkable theory.

But creationists haven't done themselves many favors in how they've handled the debate in the past. Sure, some of the supposed stupidity is a figment of the media's imagination. But you can spot major whoopsies in how creationists approach the issue:

You can't answer evolution if you forget what it means that God is creator.

Creationism is a whole bunch more than how you read the first few chapters of Genesis. Bible truth is always lived truth. So if you really mean "God is the creator," you've also got to say "God is *my* creator." If you talk about God as the creator but don't live like you belong to the owner of the universe, then your flaky or downright sinful life weakens your position. People watch you and wonder, "Does that belief work? Does it matter?" They can answer "yep" or "apparently not." Being a creationist means you live like you're God's creature, made by Him for a purpose.

You can't answer evolution if you ignore real issues.

The arguments for or against evolution can't be settled by a creationist nailing a metallic fish to her car bumper—or an evolutionist answering by gluing on a fish that's sprouted legs—or a creationist trying to trump all arguments with a fish eating the leg-sprouting Darwin critter.

There are good arguments for creationism, and there are bad arguments for creationism. Bad ones don't do us any favors. Darwinists love to hear Christians call dinosaurs demonic infestations meant to deceive us about creation. They love to grab books where a creationist engages in a "straw man argument." (The name comes from the idea of how easy it is to pummel a straw man—a scarecrow. He can't defend himself. In fact, he's not really a man in the first place, but a dressed-up bale of hay set out in the field to *look like* a real guy and scare off dumb birds who can't tell the difference. From a distance, beating up a straw man looks like a real fight, well won. Up close, you realize there was no fight at all.) You'll be unconvincing if you duck real issues and fail to represent "the other side" accurately.

You can't answer evolution if you don't speak up.

Evolutionists who *seriously* interact with the most important objections to their position are a *tiny few*. Bluster, smoke, and a few well-timed insults are usually all it takes to get the job done. Creationists—and Christians in general—aren't too great at standing up for their position by demanding intellectual integrity of their opponents. We don't, that is, tend to be the best debaters. We *should* be, since we claim to follow the One who is the truth itself. We let ourselves get walked all over.

You can't answer evolution if you're scared of the facts.

You are God's art. So is the rest of the world. That being true, there's nothing better than studying the work of your favorite artist. But loads of Christians are baffled by biology, 'fraid of physics, and avoiders of astronomy. They think studying science is going over to the dark side.

That wrongheaded fear has fed the non-Christian idea that God doesn't want anything to do with science. Lots of folks look at the world like the facts of science just are, existing just because they do. God didn't make the facts of science. Nobody did. They're just there. It's like when a mom asks her kids, "Where did these potato chip crumbs on the floor come from?" and someone says, "Nowhere . . . they just are."

To Christians, any fact that *is* a fact is a *God-fact*. Science is the study of what? The physical universe. Well, who created the physical universe? God. So you can't study God's creation without recognizing God. The "facts of science" are really nothing more than the facts of how God has put His creation together. Without factoring in God and His purposes for planet earth, you can't fully grasp the facts.

No Fear

So what does all of that have to do with poor Josh?

Lots. See, the "facts" that Mr. Kregel presents may well

be just that—facts. But facts don't exist outside the framework we use to understand them. We tuck them into a context of what we think we already know. We explain how they connect to each other. So if Mr. Kregel takes facts and straps them into the framework of how he looks at the world—and if Mr. Kregel's worldview *assumes* evolution is true and a creator *cannot* exist or *cannot* be involved in the world in any way—it's no big surprise when he concludes that evolution is the only way to go.

But is that the *only* way to look at the facts? Or are there other, better ways? Is there a more consistent way of seeing the facts, a framework that allows all the facts to be considered? Or does one system have to dismiss some facts that don't fit?

Droolin' Over DNA

Take something you've read about in school—and something we'll talk a lot about in this book: DNA. Everyone knows DNA exists. But the person who thinks as a Christian sees DNA as *a creation of God.* Another person looks at DNA as merely *a thing*—an amazing thing, to be sure, but just a thing that may or may not have existed. You can't ask that person questions about purpose, since DNA—and all stuff—just "is." So while we agree on the *fact* of DNA's existence, we disagree on the *why* or *meaning* of DNA's existence—what it's here for. The Christian sees it as God's creation, the other sees it as the astonishing result of random chance.

Josh's worldview as a Christian can handle *all* the facts,

since God *made* all those facts! There's no such thing as an "evolution fact." Facts are facts. A Christian not only can explain *why* facts are facts (they are made and defined by God), but he can then show how those facts relate to one another in a way that testifies to the truth of God (His existence, His handiwork in creation, His care for the world).

We're not saying we have all the answers.

Then again, we *are* saying we have better, more complete answers.

Stuff This in Your Backpack

Having a tight grip on these facts doesn't mean people will fall at Josh's feet begging for him to demonstrate his case. Most people who think differently simply dismiss the claims of the Bible and the facts of life that don't fit their worldview.

But you can still offer your friends that "one good reason."

You'll only make good on that chance when you know evolution at least as well as your friend knows it. Knowing what he believes, why he believes it, and how he'll argue his side takes double the work, but that's the real way to get to the truth.

And it's how *you* avoid hopping a train to nowhere.

You need to know what evolutionists believe and why. To be able to communicate with people soaked in evolutionary theory, you need to focus your attention on biggie topics like *genetics* and *natural selection*. You *must* be able to speak their language, understand their arguments, and interact with them in a way that respectfully challenges both their use of the facts and the conclusions they draw.

That's what this book will teach you.

So grab your goggles.

Ignite those bunsen burners.

And get set for science class.

Study Questions

1. What do you think about evolution? What do you think you're *supposed* to think? Who says? If there's a difference between what you think and what people say you should think, what is it?
2. What are four key differences between creationism and evolutionary theory? What does the dispute between the two ideas boil down to?
3. Why not weld together creationism and evolution?
4. What bad stuff could you do that would get in the way of giving your friends "one good reason" to consider creation?

CHAPTER 2

The Rat in the Snake

"Nature has no mercy at all. Nature says, 'I'm going to snow. If you have on a bikini and no snowshoes, that's tough. I am going to snow anyway.'"

MAYA ANGELOU
American Author
Conversations with Maya
Angelou (1989)

It was a dark and stormy day in second grade when your teacher lined up you and your fellow inmates for a spelloff. It's BYOW—bring your own word—and your opponent challenges you—*gasp*—to spell the word *bicycle*. You start with *b*. You know that somewhere it's got a *y* and an *i* and what sounds like an *s* and a *k* and an *l* but does that go before or after the *e*? Completely baffled, you crumble in a heap of confusion and take your place at the bottom of the class. A week later the same kid shows up knowing how to spell *Mississippi*. Then *Chattahoochee*. And *Okefenokee*. By the time you figure out that this kid's mom makes him memorize long words before he can have dinner, he unrolls Mary Poppins' *supercalifragilisticexpialidocious,* a word ruled out of bounds for not being in the dictionary. Unperturbed, he unfurls *antidisestablishmentarianism.*

Big words make people sound smart.

That kind of voluminosity, er, bigness of words, implies a person knows something no one else knows. Take, for example, all those *-ology* words you learn at school. Sure, you know *biology, sociology,* and *psychology*—the study of bios, socios, and psychos. But how about *entomology* (sounds like ants or aunts—but it's the study of insects). Or *paleontology* (the study of pale Minnesotans in the winter—or of fossilized plants and animals—whatever). *Herpetology* (the study of herpes—or reptiles and amphibians—you pick). Maybe you know *ornithology.* (An ornithologist down south once told Kevin's family they should check out the "bards on thuh buh-eech." Singers on the shore? How cultural! Then the ornithologist flapped his arms and said, "Bards, yah know, thah flah.") And finally, *phrenology* (the study of bumps on your head), which is not to be confused with *pharmacology* (the study of cows, pigs, and sheep—whoops, *drugs*).

Outsiders trust that all those 'ologists know what they're talking about.

We get wowed and browbeat by big words. But most of the time people who use humungous heaps of words make a subject sound *really* heavy when in fact they could say the same thing in itsy bitsy words.

Can You Spell Neodarwinianmicro-mutationalevolutionarytheory?

Here's a good example: Neo-Darwinian Micro-mutational Evolutionary Theory (NDMMET for short). Talk about a mouthful! But it's just a big-worded way of describing the currently popular theory of origins being taught in most universities, colleges, and high schools around the world. It's another way of saying "the brand of evolution begun by Darwin," but with a little more kick. Let's take it apart and see what it means:

Neo-Darwinian

Charles Darwin (1809–1892) lived a long time ago. While his basic idea is still pretty much the center of evolutionary theory, we've learned a lot since his day. Modern evolutionists have refined his ideas, so that today's evolutionary theory isn't exactly as he taught it. Instead of "Darwinian" it's now "neo-Darwinian," which means "sorta-Darwin but not exactly."

Philosophers and scientists way back to the ancient Greeks supposed that species might change over time into new, different creatures. Darwin's major fresh thought was his suggestion that a mechanism of "natural selection" was behind the gradual, ongoing change he saw as the cause of the wild diversity of all living things. We'll look at natural selection in chapter three, but here's the quick scoop: Within any species, Darwin pointed out, there is variation. The individuals in a species best adapted to their environment—those who run faster, jump higher, catch more food, and do better on standardized tests—pass their superior genes on to their offspring, who begin to outnumber their less-adapted cousins. Those individuals less fitted for the environment are weeded out, losing both in the lunchroom line and in scoring dates to prom. In time, "survival of the fittest" causes beneficial changes to spread throughout a population, whether sweetpeas, poodles, or people. In Darwin's world, it's how evolution happens.

An aside: Darwin told the world about his theory in a paper presented in 1858, the same time a naturalist named Alfred Russell Wallace announced his theory of natural selection. If Darwin hadn't beat Wallace to the publishing punch with his book *On the Origin of Species* in 1859, you might be studying "neo-Wallacism."

Micro-mutational

This is the biggie. You know the first part—*micro*, meaning *really little*—as in microwave, microprocessor, and, of course, Microsoft. Merge "micro" with "mutational" and what you get is the idea that evolution is based on small changes in the genetic code of living critters. We'll talk about mutations in chapter four, but the key is itty-bitty, teeny-tiny. Not big leaps but baby steps, micro-changes in the genetic codes that make them just a *little bit* different than they were before and make the creatures who possess them just a *little bit* different than they were before. As we'll see, there's a reason for insisting on the micro-mutation thing, because getting mondo-mutations is next to impossible.

Mutations aren't as freakazoid as they sound. Even though radiation, high temperatures, and chemicals—as well as prolonged exposure to the socks of unshowered high school boys—can cause mutations, evolutionary theory depends on both the normal variation in genes in a species as well as the routine mistakes that happen when genes duplicate themselves.

Micro-mutations are a big part of why "Darwinism" is now "neo-Darwinism." Darwin theorized about natural selection. But genetics didn't really arise as a field until after Darwin's death, and molecular biology until just a few decades ago. Later scientists tied together natural selection and mutationism with other findings from zoology and paleontology and called it "synthetic theory," or NDMMET.

Evolutionary Theory

All those changes add up to what you've been hearing about all along: evolution. That's the package of processes said to have caused life to originate, develop, and diversify on planet earth. Darwin himself spread the idea that all living things ultimately descended from a common ancestor, and he said that those evolutionary changes would be traceable through fossils all the way from ancient single cells to today's living human beings, plants, and animals.

Well, a theory is *supposed* to be a proposed explanation open to correction. Truthfully, evolution is no longer open to questioning or change, at least at the level of its most basic assumptions.

It's a huge jump to go from the facts we can all agree on—the diversity of life, and the similarities in structure and genetics seen across "family lines" in the entire plant and animal kingdoms—to assume they imply all species descended from a common ancestor, "from goo to you by way of the zoo." That's a theory, a *proposed* explanation of the obvious morphological and biochemical relationships, to use some big words your biology teacher will use for "structure" and "genetics." It's also a *proposed* explanation that natural selection plus micro-mutations are the mechanism behind life's diversity.

Evolutionists, however, say that the whole shebang—diversity, relationship, descent, and mechanism—is proven fact.

Actually, there are various brands of evolution around these days (*shhhh*—that's a big secret). But Neo-Darwinian Micro-mutational Evolutionary Theory is the most popular. It has so many problems, though, that a bunch of folks have said, "Hey, that doesn't work, so it must have happened a different way." Evolutionists go out of their way to explain that any disagreements among real scientists are fine-tuning of the evolutionary theory, usually on the level of mechanism. And in their minds that's no doubt the case—to them, descent via gradual evolution is indubitably true.

Who Forgot the Fossils?

Here's the problem. If evolution went along at a snail's pace, we should find in the fossil record—the collection of dead plants and animals forever frozen in stone—all sorts of "transitional forms," critters developing in a tiny-step-by-tiny-step march toward the species we see today. How many should we see? The number should be huge to the point of being "inconceivable," to use Darwin's own word. But those millions of transitional creatures are missing.

Scientists propose a critter here or there such as the reptile-like fossil bird *Archaeopteryx*, but most realize that a small handful doesn't cut it. When you say there were bazillions of individuals representing millions of species and you only find half a dozen fossils you *think* fit the category, well, it's obviously a lot easier to say those half dozen have another explanation than to try to explain the missing multitude.

Evolutionists point out that you can't expect the fossil record to be perfect. After all, only certain things fossilize and only under certain conditions, so the fossil record maybe looks more like snapshots than a movie. Yet saying "All those transitional forms existed but we can't see them" is like letting a three-year-old color pictures of imaginary relatives to fill blank pages in the family photo album. It's not the same thing as evidence. And other proposed transitional forms have turned out to be bad excuses, like the *Neanderthal* man and *Cro-Magnon* man that not long ago were cited as "missing links" between apes and us. They turned out to be subspecies or nonexistent categories, a big shrink of missing links.

Creationists spend a lot of time pointing at the fossil record. But it doesn't do a lot of good to argue with people and shout "Show me the bones!" because evolutionists assume their evidence exists out there somewhere. Besides that, there *are* evolutionists who realize we don't find what we *should* find if the NDMMET brand of evolutionary theory were true. They offer alternate explanations.

Meet the Competition

Scientists in a variety of disciplines have realized huge objections can be raised to Neo-Darwinian Micro-mutational Evolutionary Theory, so they've come up with other ways of working stuff out.

One or two scientists who admit fossils don't show NDMMET have proposed that instead of the itsy-bitsy, teeny-weeny steps of NDMMET, what really happened was big, humungo leaps, similar to a lizard laying an egg and *poofo!* out cometh a bird. Scientists call this sudden appearance of new species "saltationism," laughing it off as a "hopeful monster" theory, like your parents wanting a human baby and instead birthing an advanced alien lifeform. Saltationism is rejected by most evolutionists for no little reason—it's a genetic impossibility—but they no doubt also think it reeks of the sudden emergence of species that creationists contend for.

Punk Eek!

A more popular alternative to NDMMET has been advanced by Stephen Jay Gould and others. "Punctuated equilibrium" says evolution takes place relatively rapidly—and in smallish, out-of-the-way places. When those newly evolved, beefed-up critters from the backlands wander into an area populated by older, less-developed species, they quickly replace them.

Punctuated equilibrium tries to explain why we don't find transitional forms we'd expect; paleontologists only dig, after all, in a tiny percentage of the land available for breeding crops of mutants, so it would be unlikely they'd stumble on the particular area where the evolution of a particular family of critters took place (especially if it was in your backyard and the sacred spot is covered up by your old sandbox). Evolutionists who reject punctuated equilibrium argue it doesn't give adequate time for new species to evolve. And we think it's a nice way of saying "We can't find the transitional forms, but that's because all the evolution took place in little places we'll never find." It doesn't seem a lot more believable than "I did my homework but I left it at home."

You might wonder about why someone would suggest a theory that says "Don't ask me for evidence. My theory doesn't require any." Well, it's simple. Once your worldview dispenses with a creator and demands belief in evolution, you'll propose whatever it takes to keep that belief intact. Even scientists are slaves to their worldview, know it or not.

Regardless of competitors, NDMMET is the big idea being squished into your head whenever you watch TV, listen to the radio, or read biology books. Life as we see it today, evolutionists say, got here by a process that involved tiny changes over *untiny* amounts of time. And tuck this in your head for our discussions later in the book: These *must* be *single steps* to work.

This Car Ain't Got No Driver

Picture this. It's February, and you're freezing your fandango in Minnesota, where winter practically starts in

September. You're hankering for "a land of seemingly limitless space and tremendous vistas, sun-swept mountains and valleys, lofty plateaus, narrow canyons, and awestriking stretches of desert."

You've read the tourist brochures. Your soul cries out. You want to go to Arizona.

Now tell the truth: Wouldn't you be weirdly amazed if you fueled up your car in Minneapolis, slapped a brick on the gas pedal, climbed in the backseat, and found a few days later that you and your car had shown up unaided in Phoenix?

NDMMET is like that. It's a car zigging and zagging its way down the road without a driver. No direction. No one in charge. Completely clueless. Random. Purposeless. Without design. You'll wind up somewhere. But surely not where you intended. It's hopping in the backseat and hoping for the best.

So Why Is This a Problem?

In the next couple of chapters we'll really dig into how NDMMET works—or doesn't.

But one last thing to think about before we move on is what evolution says about meaning—what it implies about the universe and your place in it.

Compare it to finding out your birth wasn't quite planned.

The younger and better looking of the two authors of this book was—how can we put this delicately—an accident. He didn't know that fact until his late 20s. And he didn't think much about it until he was teased silly about it by his wife.

Being the baby of the family who arrives with less than the ideal spacing his parents might have wished is a fact you can live with—when you're born into a family where you're loved, that is. You could also wind up wondering if you were wanted.

Evolution isn't just "You were an accident" but "We're all an accident." And there's no one waiting on the homefront to love us.

Evolution is all about random accidents. It has no destination, no goal it works toward. What is—just is—because it is. Read that again. Evolution can't offer answers to deep questions like "Why are things the way they are?" Everything is just how it happened to happen. Nothing more.

People who believe in NDMMET don't have to think hard to come up with the idea that there's no ultimate reason for living. They easily fall into ideas that only the best and brightest people in this world have a right to exist, as we'll see briefly at the start of the next chapter. Once you abandon God as the creator and embrace something like NDMMET, your life is just the result of random forces beyond your control. They weren't headed anywhere when you got here and aren't going anywhere after you leave. You're alone in nature's rough, tough world, just you and the other crazy animals. And like Maya Angelou said at the start of this chapter, nature isn't always a cozy spot.

That Won't Persuade Anyone

Remember how we said it doesn't do much good to talk to evolutionists about fossils? Don't be surprised if your teachers or friends blow off this part of the debate, too. "That's not the issue. Who cares?" they might say. But saying the world is a zany ball of purposeless dust hurtling through space, going nowhere, coming from nowhere, with no goal, no end in sight, the result of mere random chance—that's heavy-duty stuff. It impacts how you think about yourself, your life, everything. NDMMET isn't just a scientific theory content to sit over in the science department and not badger the rest of life. Nope. It walks right out of the area of science and says to sociology, psychology, anthropology, and the daily stuff of your human life, "I'm here, I'm bad, and I rule."

The Rat in the Snake

We've been arguing that there's a better explanation to what we see in the world: God's design. And it's the opposite of randomness.

Why is this important? Like we mentioned in chapter one, some Christians embrace the evolutionary theory but say that God nudged things along in the right direction. But real evolutionists say that's not what happened. *The evolutionary theory developed out of a worldview that has chance as its god.* Random chance is the ultimate decision-maker in evolutionary thinking, and that's why evolution just doesn't fit with Christian thinking at all. There's no room for the Christian God.

The evolutionary theory asks that you accept a tightly wrapped package. It includes facts we can all accept, like the jaw-dropping diversity of life. But it's wrapped up with nasty stuff like descent, evolution—and ultimately atheism.

You're the snake.

NDMMET is the rat.

You're supposed to swallow it whole.

Science With the Lights On

We like science. James bred about a million fruit flies in genetics studies in college before completing a major in biology and evolving into a theologian. While still in high school Kevin held a full-time adult job as a lab tech. And he conducted his own small-scale experiment feeding treated sewer water to lab mice, proving what common sense could tell you—that mice shall not live by sewage alone.

You maybe like science, too.

But science can't tell you everything.

In chapter one we mentioned the rules science sets for itself. Science elbows God out of its explanations. When you start with an assumption that God isn't involved, you *must* find a natural answer. No matter how bad your explanation, you dismiss God and keep telling the same silly story.

To us that seems like exploring a cave without a lantern. You might touch the roughness of the walls, feel the brush of a bat, hear the trickle of water. But because of the darkness you could stand nose-to-nose with a stalactite and not see it. You'd be missing important facts.

We don't claim to see God. But we aim to turn on the lights to spot the effect of His work. This is science with the lights on, allowing for the possibility of God's involvement. In the rest of *What's With the Mutant in the Microscope?* we'll be pointing out five "Facts of Life," things science has discovered that point to design—and a designer.

Now that we've outlined the basics of evolution, we'll check out the scientific facts in depth. We'll see if they point to something other than what the evolutionary theory claims. For starters, we'll peel apart natural selection and mutations, then look at cells, DNA, and the irreducible complexity of life.

Guess what?

We'll find exactly what you'd expect in a created universe.

Study Questions

1. What's the meaning of each piece in the term "Neo-Darwinian Micro-mutational Evolutionary Theory" (NDMMET)?
2. What good does it do to talk about fossils with an evolutionist? Why?
3. Why is it a big deal that evolution is purposeless (based on dumb luck)?
4. Is it possible to do "science with the lights on"? What would a scientist say?

CHAPTER

He Who Has the Most Kids Wins

"Nature is not interested one way or the other in suffering, unless it affects the survival of DNA."

RICHARD DAWKINS
British Biologist
River Out of Eden (1995)

In the interest of advancing the human species, we'd like to propose an experiment. For the next several hundred years or so we would like to encourage the exclusive, selective breeding of people possessing two genetic variations, specifically (1) big ears and (2) the ability to wiggle those ears. We think it behooves the human race to restrict the marrying and baby-making of such people solely to their own kind, with the goal of rapidly producing a breed of humans able to fly, henceforth known as *homo sapien earflapicus mightysplendiferous*. Interested persons should submit ear measurements and a video recording demonstrating their ear-wiggling skill to us at . . .

Well, maybe not.

But it almost makes sense. Maybe in a millennium

we'd have a race that soars like Disney's Dumbo. Please note that we're not poking fun at ear-wigglers or people with larger-than-average auditory orifice flaps. Our guess is that they'd take over the planet.

Our proposal isn't all that different from the suggestions of people who wanted to use deliberate selection to improve the stock of the human race—encouraging the breeding of people who looked like Barbie and Ken dolls and outright banning unfit types such as criminals and the mentally handicapped.

No joke.

This "eugenics" movement began in England with Sir Francis Galton, a cousin of Charles Darwin set on encouraging the stupendous smarts he saw in his family. Eugenics spread to the U.S., and in 1924 the federal government enacted a law severely restricting immigration from eastern and southern Europe, whose peoples were said to be polluting "pure" Americans. By 1930 some twenty-four American states had passed laws aimed at sterilizing social misfits and banning interracial marriages. Sweden stopped its eugenics program only in 1976—after the forced sterilization of more than sixty thousand "inferior" people, including people of mixed race and poor eyesight, most of them female and many of them teenagers. But this over-the-top "social Darwinism" was most brutally fulfilled in Adolf Hitler's attempts to build a master race prior to and during World War II.

Hmmm . . .

Getting to Know Natural Selection

For thousands of years people have noticed they could breed plants, animals, and people for desirable characteristics. From a generic dog, for example, they produced varieties from the size of a rat to the size of a well-fed fourth grader.

Charles Darwin suggested the same thing was happening—unguided—in nature.

Got that?

The same diversity that the brains of breeders accomplish through *artificial selection*, Darwin said, is what happens in nature through unthinking, unintelligent forces. Even so, Darwin's name for this process—natural selection—is a term creationists can put to good use.

Why would we like natural selection when we disagree with Darwin's theory?

For starters, the phrase is so entrenched in science that there's no reason to fight it. And now get this: Natural selection is one of the greatest proofs of God's role in creation around. So why argue about terminology?

Most evolutionists just fainted at the claim that natural selection is a distinctly creationist fact. But hear us out. You'll see what we mean.

Sometimes natural selection is called by another name—micro-evolution—and that can be really confusing. *Micro*-evolution means change on a small scale (finches with different-sized beaks, for example, coming from an original pair of mom and dad finches). *Macro*-evolution means change on a big scale (lizards evolving into birds, for example). What's even more confusing is that we can agree that micro-evolution takes place even though we deny that macro-evolution happens to happen.

A Flock of Gleeds

Don't know what a gleed is? Good. No one does. If you do, you're goofier than we are. But for the sake of getting a handle on natural selection, let's make up a critter of our own:

The gleed is a small bird that lives in forested areas of, say, North America.

It weighs about a pound, bulky for a bird.

It eats bugs. (What else would a gleed eat?)

It's pretty fast, so only fast critters prey on it.

It's normally brown, with yellow highlights on its wings. You have to imagine the brown and yellow since this book is black and white. Here's a standard, happy gleed:

Gleednorm

Now, why create a whole new species? Because with the help of our imaginary gleeds we can illustrate the most important elements of natural selection.

You see, a population of gleeds—or any other critter—exists in an environment. Those surroundings determine how many gleeds can survive in an area. Obviously, the two biggest factors are (1) food and (2) predators. You need enough food to survive and feed your offspring, and you can't have too many predators munching on you and the kiddies. There's a balance, though. If you have too *much* food available for your gleeds, you end up with a growing flock of fat gleeds who eat up all the food—and a bunch of them then die off. Not good. And if you have too *few* predators the gleeds get out of hand and again eat up all the food—and starve.

Say it with us—*balance. Baaah-laaaance.* Food, but not too little or too much. Predators, but not too few or too many.

Other factors impact how much food is around, like rain, temperature, forest fires, you name it. The same factors and others probably affect how many predators lurk in the shadows ready to munch you. It's actually a complex system of checks and balances, with each population impacting others.

All of Mama's Gleeds

With these things in mind, let's think more deeply about our flock of gleeds.

A mama gleed can tell all her little gleeds apart. She knows that not every gleed looks exactly like every other gleed. Some are a little lighter, some a little heavier. Some are a little taller, some a little shorter, some a little faster, some a little slower. Some have more yellow on their wings. Some have wings colored a brighter yellow. Each is an individual, each a little different from all other gleeds.

If we plot all these characteristics on a chart, it'd look something like this:

Genetic Spectrum Graph

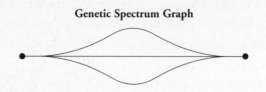

Most gleeds would be close to the middle of the population—close to average height, weight, speed, color, etc. Just like people your age. There's an average that pretty well describes most. But there are always some who are a little taller and a very few who are a *lot* taller, and some who are a little shorter and a very few who are a *lot* shorter.

That handy graph pictures what's called the "genetic spectrum," the range of various body types present in the genetic makeup of our population of gleeds. The various body types are technically called "phenotypes," and the genetic "coding" for each phenotype is called a "genotype." The genetic spectrum allows variations within our herd of gleeds, variations that come to light with each new generation of gleeds. Like people, gleeds get half their genes from Mom and half from Dad.

We'll see in a moment why that's incredibly important. If a gleed was a gleed was a gleed—if all gleeds were exactly the same and there was no variation—the gleeds and all the rest of us breeding beings would be in deep trouble.

Here is a gleed from the shallow end of the gene pool:

You see, as long as everything stays the same, the center point in our genetic spectrum won't move much over time. Gleeds will be gleeds as long as . . .

. . . the number of predators stays within the same

range—whoops! Can you smell something coming? A rift in the storyline to be developed later in this chapter, perhaps?

Gleedslow

. . . predators don't develop any new, more effective ways to catch and consume gleeds—like a Kentucky Fried Gleed store on a prominent corner in the forest.

. . . the food supply remains constant—no massive departure or dying out of the gleeds' own tasty bug treats.

Then the gleed population will remain the same over time.

Dressing for Success as a Gleed

You've probably never thought about what a gleed would consider "success." But scientists know. Success in the wild world of the forest is easily defined: He who has the most kids wins. That is, a successful animal is the one who manages to have the most kids and get them through to maturity so they have kids of their own. Like Dawkins said in the quote at the beginning of the chapter, the winner is the one whose DNA survives to reproduce.

That's the secret: The better adapted you are, the more kids you produce, who will in turn survive to pass on your genes to the next generation. If your kids can get more food and avoid more predators, they will be more successful than the poor gleeds who have neon-colored wings that blink "Eat me! Eat me!" or who freeze with fright at the sight of the bug Mom just spit up for supper.

And that's why the gleeds who are at the middle of the genetic spectrum stay there; they are best suited for the environment in which they live, so they have the most kiddies. The huge point to catch here is this: Except for freak accidents, natural selection functions to maintain our flock of gleeds *in the form and shape they have today.* Natural selection, in other words, *keeps the population the same.*

How? If something changes—say, a genetic mutation, which we'll discuss below—so that you end up with a gleed way different from the rest of the gleeds, it probably won't fit its environment. It won't compete for food and dates, as well, and so is less likely to live to pass its genes on to the next generation. Natural selection weeds out the misfits and maintains the population right where it needs to be.

If you don't like the idea of a misfit gleed being weeded out, just be quiet and eat your chicken nuggets.

Why is this such a major issue? It's simple. Here is a mechanism we can observe operating in nature. Here is a mechanism the evolutionists say is the grand wonder behind evolutionary change. Yet the vast majority of the time the mechanism of natural selection doesn't *change* a species. It *conserves* a species. It's so big we can call it a Fact of Life:

Fact of Life #1

Natural selection is an observable phenomenon that normally maintains rather than changes a species.

To make natural selection the main engine of change, evolutionists have to ignore the norm and rely on the grotesquely rare exceptions!

No More Funny Stuff

Doesn't something smell funny when evolutionists focus on the exception rather than the rule? Whenever you hear evolutionists talk about natural selection, remember that they're talking—every time—about the *exception* and not the *normal* function of the mechanism!

More on that in the next chapter.

But first let's see what happens when things do change, when the environment of our happy little gleeds goes awry.

Change, Change, Everything Changes

Things change. Environments change. Droughts come. Volcanoes erupt. Rivers change course. Plagues of locusts descend upon the land. Condominiums and golf courses and strip malls get built. Stuff like that. So what happens then? That's where it gets really neat. Natural selection makes it possible for poor critters like gleeds to *adapt* to a changing environment. And here's how it works.

Let's throw a curve at our happy little flock of gleeds. After many moons of comfortable existence, the gleeds face a new group of predators foraging the forest, animals that can munch a gleed faster than a carbo-loading cyclist can finish a plate of pasta.

If gleeds were grass, the predators would be the lawn mowers.

But you knew these gleed-eaters were comin' around the mountain.

Note: No actual gleeds will be harmed in the telling of this story.

And gleed-eaters are primarily attracted to the gleeds with the most yellow on their wings. The more yellow in your wings, the more likely these new predators will see you and stifle your life.

This new environmental pressure immediately pounces on our population of gleeds. Let's look at our graph again, this time showing just the amount of yellow in gleed wings. Before our gleed-eaters showed up, here's what it looked like:

Gleedeater

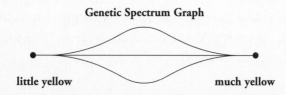

Genetic Spectrum Graph

little yellow   much yellow

Our new predators really like all the lip-smacking gleeds on the right side of the graph. They like them so much they have them over for dinner regularly. And for lunch. And breakfast. Being a gleed and getting eaten normally ruins your day, and it certainly keeps you from passing your genes on to the next generation.

So what's going to happen?

Well, if a new pressure is placed on the right side of the spectrum, the centerpoint will move to the left, *away from* the pressure. The environment will favor gleeds who have *less* yellow on their wings. They're the ones who will live long and prosper.

Remember this, though. Yellow-challenged gleeds have been a part of the population all along. This isn't something new to have a gleed with less yellow on the wing. It's just that pressures have risen that favor them, giving them an advantage they didn't have before. In other words, the *genetics* for less-colorful gleeds was always there. Evolution didn't invent anything. It's just that with new yellow-loving gleed-eaters on the loose, yellow-challenged gleeds have a factor working in their favor that gives them a big advantage over everyone else. There's no new kind of gleed, just more yellow-shy gleeds, a different population centerpoint. The genetic spectrum—the "gene pool" or the genetic variety always present in gleeds—allows for the adjustment of the population, over time, to the new situation.

Individual gleeds will suffer the slings and arrows of outrageous yellow-loving gleed-eaters, but the species will march bravely onward.

To Be or Not to Be

Of course, there's one problem: Natural selection takes time. Populations can't shift overnight. If there are enough yellow-loving gleed-eaters in the first wave to hit the forest, they may well mow down enough gleeds to wipe them out. That's why species become extinct. If an environment changes too rapidly, the population can't adjust and will be wiped out. The world, alas, will be gleedless.

Changes can involve predators, disease, or food supply—the most common change. Or changes can be environmental issues like humans encroaching on a habitat or showing up with shotguns, the method-of-death for passenger pigeons.

Since most changes are gradual, natural selection allows species to adjust and thrive. If the genetic spectrum didn't allow for adaptation, species would be wiped out all the time. *God knew what He was doing. It fits a species for long-term survival. Natural selection is exactly how we would expect God to design things to work.*

So What's the Fuss with Natural Selection and Evolution?

Are evolutionists completely crazy? Doesn't natural selection change species?

Let's go back to our flock of gleeds, prior to the predator invasion. Life is going along as it has for a long, long time. Then one fateful day a positive micro-mutation takes place as a baby gleed is conceived. The mutation doesn't adversely impact the bird. Instead, it increases a single enzyme, a single chemical that gives that one particular individual a slightly different physical result: This gleed has legs that are five millimeters *longer* than other gleeds.

And what advantage is that? Would you care if your legs were five millimeters longer?

It just so happens that in the gleedian forest, the average underbrush height is such that the new gleed has the advantage of seeing predators just a *little* sooner than the others. And as a bonus, the gleed can now run a *little* faster than it used to, making it possible for it to get airborne just a *little* quicker.

Now, this mutation gives the new gleed a *little* better chance of living to maturity, a *little* better chance of having offspring and hatching a new and improved next generation. There's no guarantee. Its competitive advantage may come to nothing; this particular gleed may get munched on before it reproduces. But let's say our gleed survives, thrives, and passes his new genetic advantage on to the next generation. Now you have more gleeds walking around with that little wonder, and more possibility of passing that advantage on to the next generation. Eventually, the center point of our genetic spectrum shifts. A better gleed has been built. Maybe even, we'll allow, a slightly different species of gleed.

That's the kind of small, micro-steps worked on by natural selection, NDMMET says, resulting in a new, slightly different gleed. The process takes a *lot* of time, since it's doubly difficult: Positive mutations are very rare. And there's no guarantee that a positive mutation will survive to the next generation, as the bearer of that mutation might well be killed by natural enemies.

But the interesting thing is how all this functions in the real world.

Pepper Moths and Flying People

When scientists scrounge around for living examples of how natural selection has produced evolution, they come up pretty much empty-handed. Of the millions upon millions of species alive right now on planet earth, they point to a handful of things like

- the rise of antibiotic-resistant bacteria;
- the population of peppered moths shifting from light-colored to dark as pollution increased in England; and
- varying beak size among finches in the Galapagos Islands.

Now that you've digested this chapter, do you notice anything? How gleed-like those examples are? Each of these happenings can be explained as the normal fluctuation of species, as population shifts favoring traits already present. Again, we'll allow that there *might* be incremental, micro-evolutionary changes that even add up over time to a slightly new species, or changes that come from micro-mutation rather than the richness of an existing gene pool. But none of these examples show that natural selection is a mechanism capable of producing new organs or new structures, what creationist Phillip Johnson calls "engineering marvels" like the wing or the eye. And none of them show anything close to evolution's ability to produce recognizably different critters.

Here's where our discussion can flip back to our opening suggestion, our plan to breed flying humans.

Even when we employ intelligent, deliberate selection over great lengths of time—like some five thousand years of breeding dogs—even when we have generation after generation of concerted effort, which is possible with species like fruit flies . . . there are genetic limits to change. Even artificial selection doesn't produce new species, and even artificial selection can't transcend genetic boundaries that keep dogs from getting as big as houses, reptiles from turning into birds, or people from sprouting winglike ears. And if artificial selection can't produce these miracles, neither can natural selection.

God's Creative Autopilot

That's a Fact of Life. Natural selection—working randomly, unintelligently—makes a poor mechanism of change. It gifts species with the ability to adapt to a changing world. And that point makes it a great testimony to the care of a creator.

In fact, we could even invent a better phrase for natural selection: *God's autopilot*. We think it's how God designed creatures to navigate the challenges of a changing environment. It's the natural mechanism God built into all living things that allows each critter family to do what God commanded at the beginning: to reproduce "after its kind" (Genesis 1:21–22). And it works!

Natural selection is a sign of God's creatorship and

wisdom, but evolutionists have pirated this truth and turned it into the engine of evolution. They've rarely been challenged to realize it's far better evidence for a designed, purposeful universe than it is for a random, purposeless place.

But natural selection is only half of NDMMET's claim to explanatory fame. We need to chat about mutations. Like natural selection, mutations are an observable phenomenon. And like natural selection, they don't usually work the way evolutionists say they do. Natural selection and mutations are like shoelaces. Alone, they do what they're supposed to. Tied together, they become wickedly dangerous.

Study Questions

1. What is "social Darwinism"? What is "eugenics"? What's the connection to evolution?
2. What is "natural selection"? How does it normally function? How does evolutionary theory need natural selection to work?
3. Why call natural selection "God's autopilot"?
4. Name some observable examples of large changes brought about by natural selection. Could you breed people to have ears that work like wings? Why or why not?

The Genes in Your Jeans

"He must pull out his own eyes, and see no creature, before he can say, he sees no God; He must be no man, and quench his reasonable soul, before he can say to himself, there is no God."

JOHN DONNE
English Poet
Eighty Sermons (1640)

For all our talk about mutations, we still haven't detailed what a mutation actually is.

Humor us now.

Since the whole theory of evolution hinges on beneficial mutations—good changes in the genetic code—you can't scrimp in understanding this area. Besides, all sorts of bizarre and beneficial research is happening in genetics, so the more you know about this life-altering topic the better able you'll be to answer challenges to your faith. And besides *that* besides, what's shockingly real is that there's hardly anywhere else where God left His bold thumbprint as visibly as in the genetic makeup of living creatures.

In NDMMET, natural selection is nothing without mutations. In chapter three we said there are limitations to what can be achieved through selection alone. You can't breed for dogs the size of elephants or—although we haven't actually tried it—develop humans who can fly, like our proposed species *homo sapien earflapicus mightysplendiferous.* That's because there's only so much variation swimming in the gene pool. As generations of sweet peas or poodles or people marry and mate, there're only so many combinations of genes that can result, like the shuffling and dealing of a deck of cards. And natural selection has a way of weeding out the weird stuff.

So to get something new you somehow have to inject something new.

The evolutionary theory doesn't posit the existence of a lunatic nurse chasing you and the rest of nature's critters with a whopper needle aiming to inject *the new you,* although genetics research kind of works like that. The big force behind the most popular theories of evolution is one thing: positive micro-mutations.

Positive, because they *add* something to the genetic makeup of a species, a something not there before, a something that gives the recipient of the mutation an added advantage that can be passed on to the next generations. Big point to remember: The mutation not only must avoid messing things up, but somehow it must add something *good.* As we'll see, that's no easy trick. It doesn't happen every day. But without going—for now—into how rare such a mutation is, let's look at how evolutionists use positive micro-mutations to make natural selection the engine of evolutionary change.

Your Bod's Brainy Micro-Computer

When you hear the word "computer," your brain likely pulls up a picture of a computer you're familiar with, like one you work on at home or school. Your brainwaves busily build images of monitors, CPUs, printers, keyboards and mice, scanners, cables, and powerstrips. You might have that computer so tweaked that everything from its wallpaper to sound scheme to cursor designs makes it feel like it has a personality. It might recognize your voice and talk back to you. But you don't treat your computer like it's alive.

Not yet.

Thinking of a computer that's actually alive—and spitting nature's kind of clock cycles inside every cell in your body—sounds weird. But that's how things work. Every cell in your body contains a computer, a molecule of mind-boggling complexity and order.

It has a long name. It's O-S-C-A-R.

Actually not. It's *deoxyribonucleic acid.*

Memorize it. It'll show up on a test someday.

But it has a nice short one, too. M-E-Y-E-R.

Nope. It's DNA.

Dexoyribonucleic acid is a molecule that's like the instruction book for building every part of you, from the proteins that make up your body to the enzymes that keep your life going. It's a staggeringly complicated system of chemical interactions. And thinking it just "happened" to come into existence by dumb luck is the greatest mind-boggler in the world. The more we learn about these things, the *less* logical NDMMET and atheism look.

You'd have to pull out your eyes to not see God in it.

But to prove that assertion we need to know our DNA.

So let's pick apart some of the stuff. Remember, we're going to talk in terms of "your" body and "your" DNA. But this stuff's in almost every cell on earth.

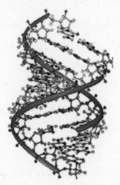

The DNA molecule is described as a "double helix," a bit of info that's helpful only if you know what a double helix is. Think of it like this. Take a long ladder—the big aluminum kind that stays the same width all the way up—and find an Aaaahnold Schwarzenegger–lookalike. Get that muscle-bound goon so mad he twists your ladder around a light pole, like stripes on a candy cane.

You are now the proud owner of a double helix, a contraption that looks like the illustration below. Not useful for getting on the roof, but a great model of what DNA looks like.

Each step that connects the two sides of the ladder is a piece of your genetic code. How do you get steps to contain information? Well, each rung of the ladder is made up of one of four substances called "nucleotides" (with the names of adenine, cytosine, guanine, and thymine, but you can remember them as A, C, G, and T). Believe it or not, your genetic code is found in simply shuffling these letters around.

How? Let's take a peek.

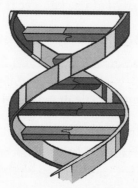

Take just one side of our double-sided twisty ladder. Here's a representation of what it looks like:

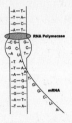

Those letters—those nucleotides—don't show up willy-nilly. They appear in triplets, happy threesomes called "codons," like AGC, GCG, UAU, and so on. The order of those threesomes is an instruction—a code—for the construction of different amino acids. Like this:

Codon	Amino Acid
GCA or GCC or GCG	Alanine
GAA or GAG	Glutamic Acid
GGA or GGC or GGG or GGU	Glycine
GTG or GTC or GTA or GTT	Valine
ATG	Methionine
TGA	End of Code

If you put on your trusty decoder ring and read the code from our twisty ladder, you get this:

GCG GAA GGA GTG ATG GCG TGA

means

Alanine, Glutamic Acid, Glycine, Valine,
Methionine, Alanine, End of Code

These chains of amino acids can have some unusual twists. They normally fold over on themselves, creating *very* specific shapes. Some of these chains—enzymes—not only *have* to have a particular amino acid sequence but a particular shape. Without that exact order and shape, the molecule is completely useless.

Before your brain gets fuzzy, here's a recap: Your DNA—your genetic code—is made up of nucleotides. Nucleotides bundle in threesomes called codons. Codons code for amino acids. (A long section of those codons, in case you're curious, is what makes up a gene.) And amino acids . . .

So what's the point of amino acids?

Cashing in on Your Genetic Code

We're going to look at DNA again in chapter six and see how your body uses all this information contained in your cellular computer to build that crazy little thing called *you*.

But for now, grab this: Amino acids aren't ends in themselves. You probably know that amino acids—there are twenty—are the basic building blocks of proteins. And proteins are the building blocks of life—the stuff that makes up the majority of the tissues in your body.

A group of amino acids chained together form a substance unlike any other. String together a bunch of amino acids and you get one protein. String together a *different* bunch of amino acids and you get a *different* protein. These chains can be hundreds and thousands of amino acids long, resulting in *highly complex* and *highly specific* substances: everything from toenails to eyeballs to brain cells to nostril hairs. The information for at least thirty thousand proteins is coded in the DNA sitting in each of your cells! Collagen, for example, composes much of your bone, skin, tendons, and cartilage. Keratin makes up your outer skin and—if you have them—your scales and feathers. Fibrinogen is what cooks up blood clotting, and myosin makes your muscles contract.

Cool, complicated stuff.

Now ponder this.

If you built a birdhouse, most birds would happily move in even if you messed up the measurements. If you built a plane, you'd want to make *really* sure you got the wings and everything else essential for flying attached just right. And if you built something as complex as a body, it could get ugly fast if you mixed up those DNA codes that produce toenails and eyeballs and brain cells and nostril hairs. You'd have a hard time seeing if you got nostril hairs growing out of your eyeballs. And all of life would be really hairy if they grew in your brain.

Beware of the Mutants

Change even one letter in the genetic code and you get a viciously different protein. The end result might be totally useless, with the new protein making no impact at all. But it may also be harmful, even fatal. If the original protein was needed for life to exist, changing that one little molecule would spell death.

Hanging in there? Good. Your genetic code must still be intact.

When the DNA code is changed, even a little bit, that's a *mutation*. A mutation can be tiny, like one letter in a sequence (the *micro-mutation* in Neo-Darwinian

WHAT'S WITH THE MUTANT IN THE MICROSCOPE?

Micro-mutational Evolutionary Theory). Or it can be huge, like changing dozens of letters around. A mutation might happen in some out-of-the-way place, like a skin cell at the end of your pinky. You hear lots about one kind of negative mutation, where a cell's genetic material gets messed up and the cell starts duplicating itself uncontrollably. That's called cancer.

But big or small, if a mutation takes place in your reproductive cells—the cells that determine the genetic code passed on to your offspring—that's a mutation that's vitally important. In fact, for evolutionists, changes in those genes in your jeans are the only ones that matter, since it is only those micro-mutations that can create "new and improved" baby critters, like a flying human or a slightly longer-legged gleed.

One Wrong Notch and I'll Throw You Away

Are you pondering what we're pondering?

If you're thinking hard about all this, you've probably already figured out that if you have a code that's incredibly long and the end result of that code is incredibly specific, playing around with even a little bit of that code has got to be a messy thing. It's like having a key for a lock that's three feet long, with countless little spikes and gnarls and gulleys on it. You take the key to get it duplicated, but when you bring it home it won't open the lock. All it takes is a tiny mistake between your old key and the new key, and it won't work. Close doesn't count.

One-change-and-it-won't-work is even more true with the long chain of amino acids that make up a protein. Change just *one* molecule and *snap!crackle!pop!* it's something completely different. Its shape might be altered, its properties changed. *Something* ends up different, and the resulting substance, like our slightly wrong key, won't do its job.

Doubly Gnarly Mutations

Want to see a few more curve balls the evolutionist has to hit?

Take this: Sometimes the same section of DNA actually codes for *two* different things. In our sample, for example, we could have started reading the section at a different point on the line. Instead of starting with "GCG," what if we broke it up differently and started with the C instead of the G? Now each codon is different, and each codes for something else. That kind of thing happens in nature! And now imagine changing just one letter in that code: It messes up not *one* substance, but *two*! Such a mutation would have double the impact and has twice the chance of messing things up.

Mutants Don't Live in Sewers

So if that's a mutation, what's a mutant? It's a critter carrying mutated DNA.

From what you see on TV you'd think that mutants are either pizza-scarfing Ninja Turtles or grotesque thingies crawling out of a nuclear waste dump.

Fact is, the *vast* majority of real mutants never see the light of day. The changes in their genetic code most of the time have one result—death—because most of the time a mutation majorly disrupts the production of proteins *absolutely* necessary for life. So most mutants are goners before they are ever born. Put it like this: If you were a mutant, you wouldn't wind up looking like you crawled out of a sewer. You wouldn't crawl out of a sewer. You'd be dead.

Those kind of mutants are the stuff of science fiction. NDMMET uses the term *micro-mutational.*

Those teeny-tiny mutations in the genetic code don't result in the critter looking like a monster from a low-budget movie. And *most* mutations are "teeny" by nature: Massive reshuffling of the genetic code is rare. But the news isn't any better for micro-mutants. In the vast majority of instances, even micro-mutations don't build a better gleed. They're deadly, or if the critter survives, they're what biologists call *deleterious*—harmful. They *take something away.*

Fact of Life #2

Exact reproduction of genetic material is necessary for the survival of a species, and mutations are almost always harmful or deadly.

A recipient of a micro-mutation is—almost all the time—*less* than his brothers and sisters. A gleed with a micro-mutation is—almost all of the time—*less* likely to be able to compete with normal gleeds. There's a whole lot of micro-mutating going in the DNA of earth's critters. But hardly any of it is positive.

Coming Up With a Good Mutation

Think of it like this: Your genetic code is even more complex than the computer code that makes up your all-time beloved video game. If you take a magnet and rub it all over a hard drive or all over a magnetic game cartridge, you'll create a do-it-yourself mutation of computer code. You rewrite stuff. And the result is a royal mess. Your data gets funky, your game freezes up and dies and—worst of all—your high scores and save points go up in magnetic smoke.

Imagine if all the adolescent boys in the history of the universe skipped school and spent their days rubbing magnets on their favorite video game cartridges. Would you expect an incredible game to be produced? Would Donkey Kong 2 evolve into Donkey Kong 3? Could the magnet-rubbing boys—at the least—make new levels appear?

The odds of beneficial changes to the computer code being created at random can be calculated mathematically. They're almost nil. It's about the same likelihood of all the molecules in a cow moving together to make it jump over the moon—or of all the atoms in a statue jostling in the same direction so that the statue of the Virgin Mary in your neighbor's lawn waves at you.

Evolutionists argue that the odds for positive mutations must not be so scary—the calculations must be wrong—because life, after all, is here. It, after all, has evolved. (Notice those presuppositions?) It's that almost-nil level of chance that NDMMET turns into *the* answer for how all of life has developed. Those impossible events, their theory says, have happened not once, not twice, but millions of times over to step-by-step produce the millions of non-interbreeding species on planet earth.

By the way, life is a living laboratory. There are now six billion human beings on the planet, more humanoids than have walked the planet at all other centuries combined. If it's true that far fewer opportunities for evolution brought us from ape-like to upright, we should be seeing hearty new humanoids evolving all around us. Email us if you spot anyone unusual. Better yet, email the FBI, CIA, NSA, and MIB. Or the *National Enquirer*.

The Evolutionists' Challenge

We'll look more at these issues later on because we haven't even touched on the real wonders of the genetic system, like how a brainless cell can figure out how to read DNA, put together proteins, and truck them around inside itself or export them to other places. But just this small bit of information helps us see the tremendous challenge evolutionists face in making NDMMET work.

Think about it.

These evolutionists have *faith*!

It's pretty weird thinking this death-defying, life-producing marvel happens in our bodies every second. But it does.

It's a whole lot weirder to imagine the whole system just sorta invented itself by random chance. But evolutionists do.

How trusting do you have to be to believe that all of life's complexity is the result of dumb luck, of random positive mutations—mutations that occur one at a time, manage not to kill the critter that carries them, and survive all the predators in the wild so they're passed on to the next generation?

Here's how we see how evolution's theory of natural selection plus micro-mutations are like shoelaces gone twisted. A shoelace doing its own thing on its own shoe is just great, just like natural selection and micro-mutations are each real, observable phenomenon in the world. Tied together, they produce a system that works *doubly* against change, not one set up to happily produce millions of distinct species:

- Natural selection works to maintain a population at its center point.
- Almost all of the time a genetic mutation is harmful or fatal because it produces a new, potentially deadly substance while junking old parts of a critter necessary for life.

And again, when we flip on the lights we can see a sign of God's design. He designed critters great and small with a system to reproduce themselves. God programmed us to survive and flourish through the wonder of the genetic code. And He built in a quality-control system that guards against corruption.

But there's more evidence of design.

Read on.

Study Questions

1. What does DNA look like? What are its parts? How do they work together to make life happen?
2. What's a mutation?
3. When mutations happen, what usually results? How hard is it to come up with a positive micro-mutation?
4. How are the evolutionary theory's twin truths of natural selection and micro-mutations like two shoelaces tied together?

CHAPTER 5

The So-Called Simple Cell

"Here we are, we're alone in the universe, there's no God, it just seems that it all began by something as simple as sunlight striking on a piece of rock. . . . We've only got ourselves."

JOHN OSBORNE
British Playwright
Jean in The Entertainer (1957)

You've probably had it tossed at you: "Scientists have proven that life could arise from non-living matter due to random inputs of energy, probably in the form of lightning, producing complex amino acids. These amino acids are the building blocks of life, and as they gathered together, they formed the first primitive cell."

Maybe you didn't hear it in those exact terms, but we've all had the idea drummed into our heads that life sprang into being as simple, single cells. If you're a Trekkie, you might remember the puddle-of-primordial-goo scene in the final episode of *Star Trek: The Next Generation*. The cosmic villain known as *Q* takes Captain Jean-Luc Picard back to the earliest period of earth's existence. And right there—bubbling at Picard's feet—the first life on earth was about to evolve. Q interferes, and it doesn't evolve. At least until Picard saves the day.

The story we're all led to take as truth is that a bunch of chemicals made friends and became a single cell. That's good news for evolutionists because their theory needs a single reproducing cell before lively things like mutations and natural selection can happen.

Those simple little teeny-tiny cells—that's how it all began.

Or so they say.

The Puddle at Picard's Feet

In the 1950s, scientists Stanley Miller and Harold Urey produced two amino acids by jolting electricity through gases thought to be abundant in the earth's early atmosphere. Ingenious stuff. Except for three details:

- The conditions they set up didn't accurately mimic earth's conditions. To be fair, Miller and Urey worked from the best data available at the time. But their results are irrelevant.
- They didn't produce life, just two very basic parts— like producing a nut and a bolt and proclaiming you've built a car.
- They did exactly the *opposite* of what evolutionists claim nature did. They used careful design and their jaw-dropping scientific intelligence to try to direct the creation of life.

Truth is, scientists have no good theory of how life started in the first place.

Scientists know that in their evolutionary scheme there had to be a predecessor to the cell, something simpler. Some say the original something able to reproduce or "replicate" itself was an RNA molecule. RNA, as we'll see, is like a partner for DNA in making proteins and enzymes. Others say the first "replicators" were crystals—orderly arrays of atoms and molecules—in mud or clay.

The fact that neither of these theories works well is seen in a desperate theory called "directed panspermia." The leading advocate of this theory, Francis Crick, is no crackpot. He was the co-discoverer of DNA. Yet he suggests that earth was seeded with the stuff of life by a dying extraterrestrial civilization.

Hello?

But it gets crazier.

What none of those theories even begin to bridge is the vast gulf between the simplicity of those pre-life parts—the stuff in the mythical "pre-biotic" soup—and the mind-boggling complexity of life's smallest unit, the cell. It's the difference between a bolt and a Mercedes Benz.

Before There Were Cell Phones, There Were Cells

It wasn't that long ago that scientists had but a vague concept of what living cells were all about. Cells were discovered in the 1600s, but the idea that cells make up all living things wasn't proposed until twenty years before Darwin's *Origin of Species*. It was in the 1920s that scientists began to fully explore and explain the functions of the fun stuff inside a cell.

And here's what they've found: The more and more we learn about cells, the more complex the picture becomes. In fact, the cell is a tremendously complex organism that continues to defy our best efforts to fully understand it. While it was once hip to view a "single cell creature" as a basic, almost simple thing, we now know differently. University of California–Berkeley professor Phillip Johnson describes it nicely: "The simplest organism capable of independent life, the prokaryote bacterial cell, is a masterpiece of miniaturized complexity that makes a spaceship seem rather low-tech."

The cells that make up all living things are tremendously complex.

They really don't look like freak accidents of nature.

Even the simplest creatures overwhelm us with order, detail, and purpose. They're marvels of design. And they defy the common claim that life could have started down the random road of evolution as a "simple cell."

A Quick Trip Through the Cell

A quick run through a cell's basic makeup will give you a good idea of just how complicated the thing is and how fantastically difficult it would be to whip one together by chance.

Think of the cell as a city. Not a wide spot in the road where you can spit from end to end, but a real city—a New York, London, or Tokyo. Our cellular city has a capitol, library, roadways, garbage dump, tunnels in and out—rigorously controlled by cops, no less—storage facilities, and even power plants. That's all in one cell, and you've got bazillions of these things in your body! Some of them are busily allowing you to read this page. Others are keeping your food digesting and your heart beating.

Little stuff like that.

Let's look at how it all works. As always, no harm will be done to an actual cell during this cellular-dissection session.

Cells look different and have different components since they perform different tasks. The cell pictured here is sort of a vanilla cell, not particularly specialized or anything. It's making its debut here in *What's With the Mutant in the Microscope?* just to illustrate how cells, in general, operate. Ladies and germs, please give a warm welcome to . . . the So-Called Simple Cell.

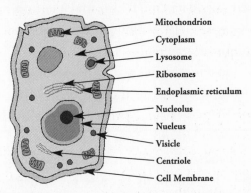

- Mitochondrion
- Cytoplasm
- Lysosome
- Ribosomes
- Endoplasmic reticulum
- Nucleolus
- Nueleus
- Visicle
- Centriole
- Cell Membrane

Don't let those long words labeling parts of the cell throw you. Scientists use long words to keep Latin teachers and textbook publishers in business. Besides, saying "endoplasmic reticulum" with a mouth full of food is a favorite pastime in labs all around the world.

Downtown City Hall

The headquarters of the cell is the nucleus, made up of the nucleolus and the nuclear membrane. Like in any big city hall these days, you have to get past security to get in or out of the nucleus. That's what the nuclear membrane does. It has doors that are heavily guarded, called "pores," although these pores aren't on your schnoz, so they don't get plugged up with blackheads and other goodies. You have to have the right ID and password to get in, which in the marvelous microworld of the cell are the proper chemical markers.

The nucleolus is a mayor's office, public library, and city planner's office squished into one. It's here you find the chromosomes—made up of DNA—that contain the information needed for most of the factories in the cell to make their products. You'll also find the info needed for constructing new city buildings, like a new endoplasmic reticulum, for example.

We'll look in chapter six at how the data stored in DNA is communicated to the rest of the cell, sort of by using a telephone system. For now let's just say that it's (1) incredibly complex and (2) defies imagination.

The nucleus, obviously, is vitally important. When a person dies, it's ultimately because his or her brain stops directing the rest of the body. The nucleus is a cell's own brainy command-and-control center. So if you nuke city hall, the rest of the city screeches to a halt. Destroy the nucleus and the cell stops working.

Factories Galore

Each cellular city has a purpose: to produce a particular product. Just like California's Silicon Valley (where hi-tech computer stuff is designed and made), the whole state of Wisconsin (nothin' beats its cheese and butter), and the middle part of Florida around Orlando (which empties wallets for fun), each cell does its own thing. Cells in your pancreas, for example, produce insulin. Cells lining your stomach cook up digestive enzymes. Cells in your eyes make chemicals needed to detect light or color. Cells in your skin might produce chemicals to protect you against ultraviolet radiation. Lots of specialized cells in the body work real hard at producing a particular protein, enzyme, fat—you name it, they make it. (Except for the stuff needed to make mouse ears. That's done in Orlando. And in the ear-making cells of mice.)

One of the cell's main manufacturing facilities is the endoplasmic reticulum. There are two kinds: rough and smooth (somebody really smart thunk that up). The rough kind has lots of ribosomes attached to it, which are produced in the nucleus and shipped out to the endoplasmic reticulum. The smooth kind doesn't have ribosomes. The rough kind produces all sorts of proteins and enzymes.

Have you noticed anything so far? Saying that these complex interactions within a cell happened by accident is like saying your Ford was put together without any intelligence designing the car, building the factory, ordering the supplies, assembling the vehicle, and shipping it to the dealership. It would be easier to believe that a blizzard blew into existence a workshop full of auto-assembling elves at the North Pole.

The Mighty Mighty Mitochondria

We'll look in the next chapter at how the ribosomes receive a message from the nucleus, telling them to produce highly specialized molecules like proteins and enzymes. We'll also see in a second how finished products get shipped out.

But we have something else to look at first. Like any factory, these things have to have *energy*. Even chemical reactions take *power*. Not electrical power, but *chemical energy*. It takes fuel to assemble proteins or enzymes. Some single-cell critters move around by themselves, and that requires power, as well.

Have you ever wondered how sucking a bladderbuster-sized Surge can get you bouncing off the walls with a sugar buzz? Well, the whole process is incredible. Even if you ignore the caffeine and skip over the enzymes that gnaw your food into basic elements, how is it your little single-cells get all that fuel and give you such a rush? What throws the switch inside a cell so it does the dance of sugar joy?

When James majored in biology in college, he got to take what are called senior boards. Boards are when you're trapped in a little room with all your professors, who take it as their solemn duty to inflict on you in two hours as much anguish as you gave them in four years. You study for months hoping to remember enough to pass.

James took his pulse while waiting his turn to enter the academic torture chamber. He found it was racing along perfectly normally for someone running in place and screaming prayers at maximum lung capacity.

Except he was sitting still.

Having managed to stay awake through three or four key classes during college, James knew he'd be asked about something called "glycolysis, the Krebs cycle, and electron chain transport." To help him study, he'd drawn the whole thing out in color markers on the board in the room where boards were held—right between the rack and the guillotine. Here's just a smidgen of what he drew:

You're probably getting the picture. There's nothing simple about this process, yet it goes on day and night in every cell between your brain and your big toe. And stupid James. Instead of making him erase it, his professors pummeled him with questions about what he'd drawn.

James knew he'd get asked about this concept because it's fundamental to how cells get their power—that is, it's a basic part of cellular respiration.

It's what takes place within the mighty mitochondria.

If you glance at the cell diagram a few pages back you'll see that mitochondria look like hot dogs with shelves. Those little shelves inside the mitochondria are where a complex series of chemical reactions take place, yielding what can only be described as the universal power source of cells, a magnificent thing called ATP.

ATP's long name is adenosine triphosphate.

Memorize it.

It'll be on a test someday right after deoxyribonucleic acid.

ATP is the gas in your tank, the stuff that makes you go.

Not *that* kind of go.

The cellular energy kind.

And the process of how a cell breaks down sugars to create ATP is what James' professors asked him about— lo, oh no, and heidi-ho—those many years ago. What James drew was just one section, the Krebs cycle.

The Krebs cycle is more complex and powerful than any Harley or Honda, yet it's only *one* section of the process your cells pull off to produce power to keep you moving—breathing, eating, thinking, living, and playing. Mitochondria, by the way, amazingly cluster where the cell needs the most juice. If a cell has a flagellum—a long, whip-like attachment used to move the cell or to move things outside the cell—you find a crowd of mitochondria at the base of the flagellum, providing power to keep things moving.

Mitochondria are a wonder of nature. Think about it: a teeny-tiny structure that produces chemical energy for living cells. How can you study them and not say "specifically designed to produce chemical energy"?

UPS, FedEx, and the USPS in Miniature

There's a potential problem back at the factories in our cell. When a factory runs full bore, there are always lots and lots of trucks, trains, and planes leaving from the factory, taking the finished products where they need to go. The same must be true of our microfactories in the cell. The endoplasmic reticulum has been cranking out specialized proteins and enzymes, but they don't do any good sitting on the cellular loading docks. They need to get out of the cell. How are they going to do that?

That's what the Golgi bodies do. Aside from having a really neato name, these structures are like mini shipping offices. These structures still aren't fully understood, but somehow—probably by molecular tags—the Golgi bodies take packets of stuff produced in the cell, sort them, determine what needs to stay in the cell and what needs to head outside, mark the packages with the proper routing slips, and send them on their way. The complex process rivals any bar-coding system used by major shippers today.

Could this all be an accident?

Think about this: Denver International Airport spent hundreds of millions of dollars to build an automatic baggage-handling system—and years fixing the system so skis and suitcases wouldn't misroute or fall out of carrying bins. If the power-lunching designers and engineers of the most modern airport in the United States couldn't easily build a system for the simple task of moving bags, how can we believe that the utterly amazing abilities of Golgi bodies are a product of dumb luck?

Demolition Experts and Micro-Terminators

Scientists have discovered that cells respond to stimulation from the outside. When the liver, for example, has to respond to a sudden influx of a chemical in the human body, liver cells rapidly build more and more endoplasmic reticuli to meet the demand.

When that need has passed, the cell can't waste energy on manufacturing plants it no longer needs. Just like a car company shuts down plants when demand falls, the cell won't keep up structures that have outlived their usefulness. You need a destruction crew to take down the old structures. And the cell has them. They're called "lysosomes."

Lysosomes are like demolition experts. They're basically smart bags of wickedly destructive enzymes. If they split open accidentally, they destroy the cell itself, like if a wrecking crew accidentally set off explosives in the middle of a city rather than at an old factory down the road.

One of the most gruesome functions of lysosomes is seen in how white blood cells work in the human body. White blood cells are like terminators floating around looking for bad guys . . . like bacteria. When they find one they engulf the thing, taking it into themselves by forming a bubble around it. Then the lysosomes attack, emptying their acidic enzymes into the bubble, devouring the bacteria in no time.

Sounds nasty.

But if your body didn't have cells like these little terminators, you'd be the one getting eaten.

The Cellular Grocery Store

Even the most unexciting stuff in a cell is incredibly complex. Cytoplasm is the watery goo that fills the space between the rest of the things we've looked at. For a long time scientists thought the cytoplasm was unimportant. They were wrong. Cytoplasm provides storage for many of the vital amino acids needed to make proteins and enzymes. Running around in the cytoplasm is a kind of messenger robots—next chapter—that track down specific amino acids, grab them, and transport them to the ribosomes for protein production. Scientists have recently found that the cytoplasm might well contain roads to organize and direct traffic.

Kewl—But So What?

Our little tour of our cellular city has been, we hope, rather educational. But what does it have to do with creation or evolution?

You've probably already figured that part out. Everything we looked at was obviously, inarguably, *designed*. You can't possibly look at how all these items function—

on a level that's inconceivably small, with all their complexity and interaction and interdependence—and not see design.

The *intricacy* of life glows as evidence to the designer of life. And that brings up our third Fact o' Life:

Fact of Life #3

The intricacy of life—
even life in its most basic form, the cell—
sure doesn't look like a product of dumb luck.
Its complexity is evidence of purposeful design.

When Darwin developed his theory, he had no way of knowing that the more we dug into living things the *more complex* they would become. His theory may sound like it works on the big level of gleeds running through the forest, but how did little powerhouses like mitochondria just happen to "develop"? Or Golgi bodies? Or lysosomes? The cell is a *system* that is complex far beyond the funkiest imaginations of Darwin or his early followers.

To imagine this stuff just *sproinnnnged* into existence through mutations and natural selection—no matter how much time you give the process—is several notches past outrageous. The *more* you learn about living things, the *less* logical the evolutionary theory looks.

The evidence for design gets even more obvious, because what goes on in cells is even more complex than what we've seen so far. How the body "reads" the DNA molecule and translates that information into complex proteins, enzymes, and hormones—all to produce you, your sister, or your best friend—is the clearest example of design you'll ever see.

If you want more evidence of design, take a look at the inner workings of DNA. It's like looking at the big, bold thumbprint of God.

Study Questions

1. Can scientists explain the origin of life? What explanations have they offered? Is it dumb for scientists to speculate about the origin of life? Why or why not?
2. What's so simple about a cell?
3. How is a cell like a city? Name some of the big parts and functions of our sample cell.
4. Why is a cell's complexity an example of design?

CHAPTER 6

Captain Protein and the Space Zombies

"Whatever the scientists may say, if we take the supernatural out of life, we leave only the unnatural."

AMELIA BARR
Anglo-American Novelist
All the Days of My Life (1913)

Hmmm . . . amazing! you think to yourself. You can actually go *through* the hill into caverns large enough for a throng of people. "Note to self," you whisper. "Investigate internal caverns. Were they formed by wind—or by water?"

The lowest levels of the caverns, however, hold the biggest mysteries of all. In a hollow several yards across is a three-dimensional duplication of the very hill whose interior you are exploring. Awestruck, one of your fellow adventurers faints against a cavern wall, triggering a rockslide. He's buried by long, cylindrical rocks, the likes of which you've never seen—smooth, hollow, and packed with two-dimensional sheets of an unknown material. "Note to self," you whisper again. "Investigate thin, flat objects with patterns that are exact replicas of the hill being explored."

What a striking coincidence. Your hill seems to have been able to replicate itself in smaller two- and three-dimensional renderings. You shiver as your team debates whether the big hill or little hills came first. After several more notes to self you ascend through other passageways to fresh air.

As you reach to push aside a crystalline swinging structure to make your way outside, you see your only indication that fellow humans have passed this way before. Etched on the structure are the letters "R-E-W-O-T-S-R-A-E-S."

Rewotsraes? What's a Rewotsraes?

You leave, contemplating mysteries as big as the hill itself.

Unlocking the Mysteries of Rewotsraes

You'd be a sad explorer to mistake Chicago's Sears Tower for a natural phenomenon, a freak of nature whipped together by wind and waves.

You'd have to try hard to miss the difference between a rock and a hot dog cart. Or between the 500-foot sand dunes on one side of Lake Michigan and a city smothered in smog on the other. You'd miss the message of the unnatural hill with 1,454-foot straight-up sides, 43,000 miles of telephone cable, 796 faucets, and who knows how many toilets: The tallest building in America is *designed*.

When we looked at the cell, we saw it. Order. Detail. Purpose.

All of us have a not-so-fuzzy feeling that tells us something is human-made. Exactly what is it our brains notice? What qualities make something look designed? "Design," says biochemist Michael Behe, "is simply the *purposeful arrangement of parts.*" In designed systems, "you see that the components of the system interact with great specificity to do something."

Well, nature is one mondocomplexo thingy after another—incredibly intricate parts interacting to do something purposeful.

If our virtual exploration of the cellular city in the last chapter didn't make it clear that living organisms—even supposedly simple ones—are majorly intricate, there's more. We've barely scratched the surface of what cells are up to and *how* they do what they do.

Watching how DNA works shows us complexity, interaction, and purpose at a whole 'nother level. It's like finding something as obviously designed as a Sears Tower—and then bumping around in the building's basement and discovering the architects' 2-D blueprints and 3-D models. Put it this way:

Fact of Life #4

DNA is a living blueprint—a plan—for how creatures are built. It's one screamin' sign of design.

Nothing shouts "There's a designer behind this stuff!" more loudly than finding a creature's construction instructions. You've not only spotted the purposeful thing but the blueprint behind it. It's proof of the purposeful construction of the purposeful thing.

RUPuzzledbyVelcro?

To be frank, learning how DNA zips and unzips and builds the stuff of life is a lot more complicated than figuring out Velcro.

But understanding DNA is crucial.

Why?

Knowledge in genetics is exploding. Detail on the contents of the human genetic code is almost daily news. And guess what? Knowing how a cell in your body goes from code in the DNA molecule to the finished product—a highly specific, highly specialized protein ready for export to elsewhere in the body—is yet another piece of obvious evidence for design. It's devastating evidence that these living things didn't arise by chance.

And you gotta wonder. When the sum total of what you put into your body consists of cheeseburgers, French fries, pop, shakes, pizza, and chips, how does your body turn that stuff into highly specialized molecules that are precise in function and complex in structure? You maybe don't have even a foggy picture of what goes on inside you. But all the complex things that make you don't just appear out of nowhere. If you slid your body under a microscope, what you'd see is a *brilliant* process going on right now all through your body.

But understanding the basic workings of DNA is crucial for another reason: You won't get through *any* biology class without discussing this topic. Which means you don't have to introduce an off-the-wall, off-task point to be able to say, "Don't you think it's strange to think that something this complex arose by chance? How would you explain its evolution step by step? Don't you see some purposeful design here?" Here you can use the information hibernating in your biology textbook to make your point. That's reason enough to spend real brainpower on this one.

Captain Protein's Secret Code Ring

Back at the start of our discussion about NDMMET we took time to look at the DNA molecule itself. Here's the basic structure:

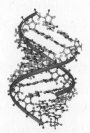

Simplifying the structure, you get

You probably remember that each rung in the ladder represents one of four substances—adenine, thymine, guanine, and cytosine—known as "nucleotides." In groups of three, these nucleotides make up a codon. Each codon codes for a particular amino acid, and amino acids are strung together to form proteins.

The DNA molecule stores a vast amount of information inside.

Go ahead—ask how much.

Well, computer technology has just a *tiny* way to go to catch up with DNA's data compression. Actually, way more than tiny. About ten thousand average-sized human cells can fit on the head of a pin, and the DNA in each of those cells could easily contain a copy of the New Testament. So DNA packs ten thousand New Testaments on the head of a pin.

That's one Harvard-bound pinhead.

But with DNA data safely tucked in the nucleus, how can the cell grab and use that information?

You need a process to read the information. What you need is the right cellular disk drive to read the DNA disk. After all, DNA is a lot like a computer disk: You can cram all the data you want on a disk, but if you don't have the right drive to read it, the data is completely useless.

The answer is again simply astounding. Here's how it works.

Life Moves Pretty Fast

"Life moves pretty fast," noted one of America's profound thinkers. "If you don't stop and look around once in a while, you could miss it." Had Ferris Bueller spent more time in school he'd realize how incredibly applicable that truth is to the study of DNA.

Life moves pretty fast indeed. The whole process you're about to witness takes less time from start to finish than it takes you to say "deoxyribonucleic acid," assuming you can say it at all.

So here, slowed down for your enjoyment, are the inner workings of DNA.

Let's start at the very beginning, which is a very good place to start.

The process of getting the information necessary for building a huge, long, complex protein molecule and transmitting it to the factories in the cell—those rough endoplasmic reticula lined with thousands and thousands of ribosomes—is called "transcription." To be brief, it involves what is technically known as "unzipping" and "zipping" the DNA molecule. And it's unzipping at *specific* points—start at the wrong place and you don't get the protein you need—then temporarily keeping it unzipped so one of the two strands can be read, and then zipping it back up again.

The DNA unzipper is called "RNA polymerase." As you've probably figured, it's a seriously specific type of substance. When it opens up or unzips the DNA molecule, a process starts that makes a new strand of material—not DNA, but a closely related substance, RNA or "ribonucleic acid." This new strand is called "mRNA," which is science-speak for "messenger RNA." This long strand is a mirror image of the strand of DNA that is being transcribed. It has the exact opposite sequence of codons—that is, it's like looking at the code in a mirror.

When the unzipper—the RNA polymerase complex—comes to a chemical marker in the genetic code, it stops the transcription process, detaches from the DNA, and floats off, possibly to go back and start the process all over again. The strand of mRNA—which may be thousands of bases long—is shuttled out of the nucleus through a pore and is directed off to a ribosome.

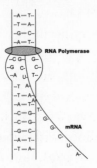

Captain Protein's Roller Coaster Decoder

You'd be amazed at how fast the next step happens, too.

You're supposed to say, "How fast is it?"

Let's just say it goes a lot faster than your grandpa can lace up his Velcro shoes.

Remember the ribosomes? A ribosome is made up of two circular units, except those units have different sizes and shapes. The larger is pretty much in the shape of a ball. The smaller one looks squished like someone stepped on it.

This is the cool part: The ribosome attaches to the mRNA molecule a lot like a roller coaster car attaches to the ride's rails. The ribosome can move along the length of the mRNA molecule, reading it as it goes along. More on that in a minute.

The next participant in this complex play is another RNA molecule with an equally fascinating name—tRNA, which is lab lingo for "transfer RNA." You might call it "gopher RNA," since that's all it does: It acts as a chemical shuttle service, but with a twist. You have to have a key to this cab to get to ride in it!

How so?

The tRNA molecule has a shape that causes it to fold over on itself, resulting in the shape in the graphic. It can attach to amino acids at the top of its stem. But most important is the fact that each tRNA molecule is "specific," which means that when tRNA goes looking to attach to an amino acid, it's only looking for a *specific* amino acid. That's because there's yet another molecule, a special enzyme that attaches only particular tRNA molecules to specific amino acids.

Think of it like this: When you're putting together a car in a big factory, all sorts of machines run around delivering parts to points on the assembly line. Scanners direct bins full of parts to the proper place. Without the right code on the label, though, the part won't get to where it's supposed to go—or worse, it gets to where it *isn't* supposed to go. Each bin is only for a certain kind of part. Put the wrong parts in and everything gets messed up.

The tRNA molecule is like one of those part-specific bins: It will only bind, because of a specific enzyme, to the amino acid that matches its "anticodon."

The anticodon is a series of three nucleotides found at the bottom of the molecule, and it's the part of the tRNA that will attach to the corresponding mRNA molecule. If the tRNA grabs the wrong protein, the entire process of transcription and translation is ruined, and you don't get the protein you need.

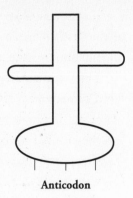

Anticodon

Creating Captain Protein

Having thoroughly fogged your mind, let's finish the process and figure out how after all of this work the cell takes a code that contains thousands and thousands of codons in the DNA molecule and turns it into a specific protein that contains thousands and thousands of amino acids in an *exact* sequence, with no mistakes.

Would you believe us if we said the process involves dozens of prepubescent DNA molecules riding their bikes really fast and yelling "Look, Mom, no hands!"?

Probably not.

Here's how it really happens:

- The mRNA molecule attaches to the ribosome.
- tRNA molecules find the proper amino acids in the cytoplasm of the cell and drag the amino acids to the ribosome.
- The first tRNA attaches its anticodon to the corresponding section of the mRNA (see the diagram below). Think about this: The anticodon of the tRNA has to

match up to the mRNA. But the mRNA is already the reverse of the DNA molecule it came from, so the anticodon is an exact match for the DNA's original code. The amino acid is exactly what the DNA called for!

- Then the next tRNA comes in, bringing its amino acid along with it.
- When that tRNA attaches to the mRNA, the first tRNA is released. But its amino acid creates a bond with the amino acid that just arrived with the new tRNA molecule.
- The next tRNA comes along, and the process is repeated.

The ribosome actually moves along the mRNA strand like that roller coaster car riding on rails, bringing in tRNA molecules as it goes along. As each tRNA latches on, the previous one lets go, but the amino acids join together, creating a longer and longer chain: the protein called for by the DNA molecule in the nucleus.

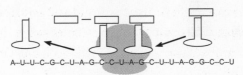

A--U--U--C--G--C--U--A--G--C--C--U--A--G--C--U--U--A--G--G--C--C--U

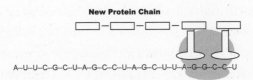

New Protein Chain

A--U--U--C--G--C--U--A--G--C--C--U--A--G--C--U--U--A--G--G--C--C--U

Protein Chain

Once the final code is reached, the last tRNA molecule breaks off and the last amino acid joins the chain. *Voila!* You have a spanking new protein. The cell packs it up and ships it off to where it needs to go, either inside or outside the cell.

Can You Say "Design"?

Now think about all the steps DNA worked through.

Are you willing to say, "That DNA transcription stuff sure looks like an accidental process to me. It's like the time I dropped twelve books for my history project into a shredder and out popped a perfectly typed twenty-page report. And you know what else? The shredder regurgitated Abraham Lincoln, too. He presented my project to the class and I got an A+. Yeah, it was just like that. A total accident."

Think of the specific, complex items needed all along the way:

- You needed a specific, complex molecule called DNA.
- You needed another very complex molecule called RNA polymerase to unzip the DNA.
- That RNA polymerase had to start and end at the *exact* point in a hugely long chain.
- You needed an accurate mRNA copy of the DNA code. A single inaccuracy and it's all over.
- You had to get the mRNA from the nucleus to the ribosome in one piece.
- The ribosome had to attach at the right spot or the code would be all messed up.

- Every single one of thousands of tRNA molecules grabbing amino acids from the cytoplasm had to get the *right* amino acid. No mix-ups allowed.
- The amino acids had to bond properly or the chain would break.
- The ribosome had to stop at the right place.
- And the cell had to get the protein to where it needed to go.

Can you say *design?* Can you imagine looking at such a process and saying, "Oh well, nobody's in charge of this. No one designed this. It invented itself."

If you can see an intelligent designer behind the Sears Tower, you surely can see a designer behind DNA. The Sears Tower, after all, is just a really high pile of concrete, steel, glass, carpet, wiring, paint, pipes, and porcelain—a dozen parts pretty much covers it. Your DNA has to worry about cooking up some thirty thousand proteins.

The Black Velvet Elvis

Design isn't all that hard to spot. Ponder what Michael Behe says: "As the *number or quality of the parts* of an interacting system increase, our judgment of design increases also and can reach certitude" (italics added). The more parts—or the better the parts—that work together in a system, the more sure you can be of design.

And if you're spotting design it doesn't make much difference whether you're looking at non-living things—like Sears Towers—or living things. Behe says that if you see a splotch of mold growing on your fridge that vaguely resembles the face of Elvis, you'd chalk that up to chance. But if a dozen molds grow in precise colors and shapes so your fridge has all the exacting artistry of a black velvet Elvis painting, you'd safely assume that your King of Rock and Roll was a product of design.

Problem is, as we've ripped through cells and DNA we've been exploring a microscopic world so unfamiliar and unreal that you might still be saying,

So? What's your point? Or

I get what you're saying about design. But I don't get the biological proofs. Or

I still feel like I don't have that 'one good reason' I can use with my friends to say why creation is real.

Even if some of the biology so far has whizzed through your brain without taking up residence, we're going to look now at one more "Fact of Life" that's easy to figure out. The biology is a little less bewildering. And the principle we'll outline is crystal clear. It's an undeniable sign of design.

See, everything we've looked at so far has been "*interactively* complex." It functions together to accomplish a purpose.

But most of it—and more examples we'll see in the next chapter—is also "*irreducibly* complex." It can't function without any one of its parts.

That's the clincher.

Let's see what that means.

Study Questions

1. How is DNA a sign of design? How is it like a blueprint?
2. How can you tell something is designed? What's Michael Behe say? How would you prove the Sears Tower shows design? How could you know if mold growing on your fridge had been shaped by human hands?
3. Why bother to understand DNA?
4. Could DNA be an accident? Why or why not?

CHAPTER
7

Amateur Autopsy

"Every formula which expresses a law of nature is a hymn of praise to God."

MARIA MITCHELL
American Astronomer
Hall of Fame Inscription (1905)

Suppose you're talking with your friends about creation and evolution. You won't be too persuasive if you say, "Just look at it, stupid! Can't you tell it's designed?" And when you talk with a teacher, you'll likely find yourself outsmarted. You probably aren't, we're guessing, a professional biologist or biochemist or anatomical expert.

You might feel like you're going to a body-expert doctor and doing a live demonstration to teach her how your innards work. You gently scalpel open your belly and poke at various globs: *Hmmm. I call this thing a "liver." But what in the livin' daylights does it do? Or this thing—that's a spleen, but I can't really 'splain that.* You'd die before you'd figure anything out. And the doctor would laugh at your science faster than you can say "amateur autopsy."

Don't try that at home.

Or at your doctor's office.

Even under anesthesia.

That situation really isn't all that different from the dawn of basic medical research. In the early 1800s a Dr. William Beaumont happened across a hapless young trapper named Alexis St. Martin, who had suffered an accidental gunshot wound to his abdomen. Mr. St. Martin's stomach protruded outside his body, covered only by a flap of skin. Dr. Beaumont's experiments on the digestive system involved tying food to a string and lowering it into . . .

Nevermind. That's a bit off task.

Here's the point: You don't have to heckle your friends or feel stupid in front of your teacher to make a solid point about creationism. Whatever your grasp of biology, you can remember the point of this chapter: Your body is *full* of systems that absolutely defy explanation by Neo-Darwinian Micro-mutational Evolutionary Theory. They're called "*irreducibly complex systems.*"

"Irreducibly" isn't as hard of a word as it looks. It's got *ir-* ("not") in front of *reduce* (to decrease) plus *-ly* (to make it an adverb so it can modify "complex"). It means "impossible to make any simpler or smaller." And here's the short version of what it means in biology: Remove any piece of an irreducibly complex system and *poofo!* the whole thing grinds to a halt.

Majorly Useful Thought: Irreducibly Complex Systems

NDMMET is mortally challenged by two related facts about living systems.

First, evolutionary theory can't explain how *interactively complex systems* arise. An *interactive system* is what we've been looking at all through this book—a biological process where a variety of parts interact with each other, play off each other, and often depend on each other. Like how cell parts get along. Or how DNA builds proteins. But that's only part of their complexity.

Second, evolutionary theory *really* can't explain how *irreducibly complex* systems arise. When a system won't work at all without *every* element present, it's called an *irreducibly complex system*. If you "reduce" it—if you remove even one itsy-bitsy part—the system stops working. You can have interactive systems that are not irreducible—they might work when some parts are pulled out—but all irreducible systems are interactive.

Let's think first about these things on a big-as-life scale.

If you have a baseball team of nine players, you have an interactive system, players working together to accomplish a goal. But it's not irreducible. You can remove a player or two and it doesn't make a ton of difference. (In fact, removing either Kevin or James from a team will *improve* performance. Well, Kevin at least.) Baseball is an irreducible system, though, when you think about *two* teams needed to play the game. Pull one out, the game halts.

Forfeit. You lose.

Or a car is a system. It's interactive, a whole bunch of parts functioning as a whole. Believe it or don't, though, you can rip out a car's stereo and the car will still run. So the car—as a whole—isn't irreducible. At some point, though, the most basic parts of a car are an irreducible system. The car won't run if you pull out the spark plug wires, for example, as the nuns in *The Sound of Music* proved when they vandalized a Nazimobile.

But that's another story.

Growing a Third Eye

How big a deal is this?

The vast majority of the systems that keep us alive and healthy are collections of components related to one another. They're *interactively* complex because their parts function together. But scads of these systems are also *irreducibly* complex: Pull out one part, they stop working. They may have two, ten, a hundred, or a thousand components. Without one, the whole thing falls apart.

And here's why this bit of info is disastrous for evolutionary theory:

Each of those parts had to evolve one by one. Remember? Evolution lives and dies on itsy-bitsy changes over time: not twenty, or ten, or five, or even two changes all at once, but single, small changes accumulating over time. The whole theory is that micro-mutations over time can produce complex living systems.

But here's a question: If you have an irreducibly complex thingy with five parts, how can evolution develop this system?

Here's the answer: It can't.

You play the mutant for a second and we'll figure this out.

Imagine that it would take five positive mutations for you to grow a third eye, say, an eye in the back of your head. That third eye would give you and your descendants multitudinous advantages, like anticipating rear-enders while driving, knowing when you're going to get jumped from behind for your lunch money, and being able to study 50% harder so you get accepted into an Ivy League college.

Remember, for a positive mutation to stick and be passed on, the mutation must give a reproductive advantage to the next generation. It's got to improve you in some way so you live and your kids live to have more kids than everyone else. And with that third eye, you and your kiddies surely would live long and prosper.

But if growing a third eye requires—*minimally*—five distinct elements to function, natural selection can't help you.

Say—by chance—that you get a positive mutation that produces one of the five elements, like the extra socket in the back of your head. Besides being outright ugly, by itself it's useless. It gives you no benefit. And you still need four more positive mutations to get the eye. By the rules of natural selection, *that mutation won't succeed in the species*, since it would be a waste of energy to produce a substance or part that has no useful purpose. Scientists recognize, in fact, that if a feature develops, provides no useful benefit, but it takes energy to make and maintain it, you and your descendents are actually at a disadvantage compared with others who don't have to waste that energy. You, your kin—and that mutation—will disappear.

Sorry. And we had such high hopes for you.

What all this means is you don't have positive mutations just hanging around waiting for other positive mutations to happen. You need all the mutations at once. And even evolutionists would call *that* a miracle. (Remember back in chapter two? They slammed that kind of miracle as a "saltation.") And the fact is, it's not just five mutations you have to wait for. It could as easily be a hundred or a thousand.

Genetic loitering isn't acceptable to your body or to your species' gene pool any more than a thousand teens hanging around a mall not spending money are to the mall owner. The cops think they're juvenile delinquents. And bust them up.

Some of Your Best Friends Are Irreducibly Complex

Several of the systems we've already looked at are irreducibly complex.

Think back to the cell. How could these things have evolved gradually, bit by bit, step by step? *It's a chicken-and-the-egg situation. Which came first? And without the other?* What good is a lysosome all by itself? What good are Golgi bodies without other structures to send their "parts" over to be packed up and shipped out? And the more we learn about these structures, the *more* complex they become! What did cells do *before* mitochondria developed?

And think about DNA. Its code is useless if you can't get at it, for example; you need RNA polymerase. You need ribosomes to synthesize protein. And ribosomes would be pretty useless items without mRNA and tRNA.

Interactive systems that require multiple parts to work present a huge challenge to modern Neo-Darwinian Micro-mutational Evolutionary Theory. Here's how huge:

Fact of Life #5

*Irreducible complexity makes it impossible
for life to have arisen and
developed by chance.
It's a sure sign of design.*

Let's look at three more examples of irreducibly complex systems that defy explanation by NDMMET but instead point to intelligent design.

Barf-o-Rama

Know what? Your stomach is a bag of barf all the time. Well, not all the time. Just when it's full of food.

If the cells lining the stomach continually pumped out maximum amounts of digestive enzymes, you'd be one uncomfortable pup. But how does your body know when to start and when to stop? And how does your body build a destructive thing like a digestive enzyme without nuking the cell itself?

Some enzymes can be safely packed up inside the cell and shipped out in tiny little bio-containers that keep the enzyme from eating the cell that's produced them. But others are too potent even for that kind of shipping container. One of those yearn-to-burn, dissolve-anything-you-eat digestive enzymes is called "pepsin."

Do you think the nice people who make Pepsi know about this?

Pepsin is just too strong to be produced in a cell in its active, food-dissolving form. So the cells along the stomach keep themselves alive in a pretty amazing way while still producing the necessary enzyme. They produce it not as *pepsin* but as *pepsinogen*, which actually sounds much more diabolical.

But it isn't.

This form has an added section of amino acids on one end that makes the enzyme inactive. Pepsinogen can't dissolve anything at all, including the host cell that produces it! Instead, it's secreted in the non-active form. Then along comes another enzyme, snips off the extra section of amino acids, and *voila*! Fully active, ready-to-refry-your-burrito-beans pepsin. Only now it's in the stomach where it belongs. Where cells are built to withstand it. And where it can't destroy the cells that make it.

This system is irreducibly complex. Without the enzyme that snips off the extra amino acids, it wouldn't work. So which came first, the inactive form of pepsin, or the enzyme that just happens to be able to snip off that extra section of amino acids? Good luck pondering that one! Darwin didn't know anything about that kind of system, and if he had he probably wouldn't have cooked up his theory.

Please Pass the Eyeballs

Creationists have long pointed to the eye as the greatest example of design in the human body. Most people reading this book are using their eyes, focusing light on the retina, which in turn is converted into chemical and biological impulses that are transmitted to the brain and interpreted as letters on a page. But the more you look into how the eye works, the more complex and obviously designed it becomes.

You've probably seen pictures like this:

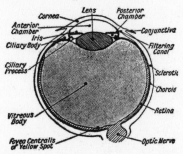

It's no secret that the eye is extraordinarily complex. But the truth is, that diagram doesn't look all that complicated. If that's all it takes to make an eyeball, you could probably build one yourself. You could get the plans on the Internet and build one in your garage. Without your parents knowing.

So let's ratchet up the magnification to the cellular/molecular level, just as we did in looking at DNA and the cell. How sight happens is way beyond what you need to know right now, but to get an idea of the eye's *real* complexity, here's *one* paragraph describing *one* stage of *one* aspect of how light focused on the retina produces an impulse that's interpreted in your brain as described by Arthur Guyton in *Human Physiology and the Mechanisms of Disease*:

> When light energy is absorbed by rhodopsin, the rhodopsin immediately begins to decompose. . . . The cause of this is photoactivation of electrons in the retinal portion of the rhodopsin, which leads to an instantaneous change of the *cis* form of retinal into an all-*trans* form. This still has the same chemical structure as the *cis* form but has a different physical structure—a straight molecule rather than a curved molecule. Because the three-dimensional orientation of the reactive sites of the all-*trans* retinal no longer fit with the orientation of the reactive sites on the protein scotopsin, it begins to pull away from the scotopsin. The immediate product is *bathorhodopsin* . . . which is a partially split combination of the all-*trans* retinal and scotopsin. However, bathorhodopsin is an extremely unstable compound and decays in small fractions of a second to *lumirhodopsin*, then to *metarhodopsin I*, then *metarhodopsin II*, and finally splitting apart to form scotopsin and all-*trans* retinal. During the process of splitting, the rods are excited, and visual signals are transmitted into the central nervous system.

You might not have the foggiest idea what all of that means. But guess what? If it didn't work, you wouldn't have been able even to see the words in that bewildering description. Thousands of times each second, this reaction takes place in your eyes, allowing you to see the difference between squiggles of black ink and the whitish paper they're printed on. And that's just *part* of the system that works together so you can see movement, light, and color. No one could guess that as we learned more and more about what happens once light hits the retina we'd discover that's the *simple* part of vision.

Problem is, the eye is a real problem for evolution because the structures and chemical reactions behind vision are irreducibly complex. Yet evolutionists say this miracle has happened more than once. Ernst Mayr has argued that the eye evolved independently—in different critters, in different times and places—at least forty times.

We wouldn't bet our eyeballs on that.

The Band-Aid Isn't Enough

You surely didn't get through childhood without falling down and getting some owies. You've cut, poked, nicked, lanced, scratched, slashed, and gashed yourself many times to cause that largest of all your organs—your skin—to bleed.

Bleeding is good.

Bleeding not only keeps bad stuff outside your body where it belongs, but it's also the first step in healing. Bleeding leads to clots, scabs, and new skin, assuming you don't get the scab wet and gooky in the shower and start the whole process over again.

But bleeding is bad.

Especially the wet, gooky scab part.

You take for granted that if you apply pressure to a cut, bandage it up, and keep it clean, it'll heal in time. Folks with the disease *hemophilia*, though, are called "bleeders" because they can't naturally stop bleeding. Their blood won't clot. Yet hemophilia is caused by the lack of a *single* critical element in a *tremendously* complex, interactive process that results in blood clotting.

But why don't we *all* have a problem that's the exact opposite of hemophilia? Once your blood starts clotting, why doesn't *all* your blood curdle? You'd turn into a bag of Jell-O if it did, but something about a cut causes the blood to know where and when to start the process and where and when to stop.

Most of the clotting process revolves around taking a plasma protein produced in the liver called *prothrombin*, and converting it to *thrombin*, its active form. Obviously, you don't want thrombin running around actively because you'd become that dreaded bag of gelatinous ooze.

But a tangled process of factors and co-factors work together to stop bleeding—not in a nice, simple, *bing-bang-boom* linear reaction, but in a twisting, turning, folded-back-on-itself series of reactions and counter-reactions that defies imagination. Remember that biology-textbook paragraph a couple of pages back about the chemical reaction that allows you to perceive light? Take that description, multiply it by ten, then shake it up and down till it's all mixed up. Then you'll have some idea of how complicated it is for blood to clot.

Starting and stopping clotting requires a tremendously

intricate system that keeps everything in balance and allows the body to be a self-sealing mechanism. Removing just one element breaks the system. And hemophiliacs are proof.

Eyeballs and Barf Bags and Scabs

The systems that make eyeballs and barf bags and scabs possible are irreducibly complex. They can't be explained by evolutionary theory without a *long* list of "Well, maybe this happened, and possibly then this, and then maybe this happened. . . ." NDMMET says a mutation has to give a competitive advantage to be preserved. But one part of an irreducibly complex system is—at best—a useless piece of equipment without the rest.

Now that you know about irreducibly complex systems, you'll spot them in every living critter, over and over and over again. And when you do, you'll see example after example that refutes NDMMET.

So how can a scientist look at these systems, fully figure them out, and yet not see *design*? That's a question we'll tackle next as we wrap up this *Tour de Mutant*. Till then, think about these words from the classic textbook *Biology*:

> One marvels at the process of evolution as exemplified by the intricate flower of an orchid, the shell of a chambered nautilus, or the opposable thumb and forefinger of the human hand. Remember that NAD (a molecule important in making coenzymes), ATP, and indeed the place of each amino acid in a poly-

peptide chain are also the products of evolution and also, you must admit, quite marvelous. Perhaps even beautiful.

Sure, those things are beautiful. But their organized, purposeful complexity, the evolutionist argues, isn't created. Unorganized purposelessness is the "designer" of such "beautiful" things. The same author said,

Now the new biology asked us to accept the proposition that, like all other organisms, we too are the products of a random process and that, as far as science can show, we are not created for any special purpose or as a part of any universal design.

Why can't someone as smart as this writer see the design all around us? Because recognizing design isn't a function of *how much you know* but *what you do with what you know*.
Seeing design is a function of worldview.
Not of raw brain power.
If your eyes see it . . .
but your mind won't accept it . . .
it's like it isn't there.

Study Questions

1. What is "irreducible complexity"? How is it different from "interactive complexity"? Is a baseball team irreducibly complex? How about a car?

2. Why is irreducible complexity a majorly useful thought? How does it make micro-mutational evolutionary theory impossible?

3. Could you grow a third eye in the back of your head by micro-mutations? Why or why not? Would you want to?

4. What three systems in your body display irreducible complexity? How do you know they are irreducibly complex?

CHAPTER 8

The God Who Gives You Toast

> "Darwinian Man, though well-behaved,
> At best is only a monkey shaved!"

W. S. GILBERT
English Librettist
Princess Ida (1884)

You've no doubt heard the legend of the blind men and the elephant. One man grabs the tail and proclaims that an elephant is just like a rope. Another bumps up against a leg and says it's like a tree trunk. A third feels the trunk and thinks it's a hose. They each have a different perspective of the same object.

But that's not the story we want to chat about.

Check out this new and improved tale of visually challenged men and an elephant from Michael Behe's book *Darwin's Black Box.* It's a bazillion times better than the old one, and it exposes a different kind of blindness:

Imagine a room in which a body lies crushed, flat as a pancake. A dozen detectives crawl around, examining the floor with magnifying glasses for any clue to the identity of the perpetrator. In the middle of the room, next to the body, stands a large gray elephant. The detectives carefully avoid bumping into the pachyderm's legs as they crawl, and never even glance at it. Over time the detectives get frustrated with their lack of progress but resolutely press on, looking even more closely at the floor. *You see, textbooks say detectives must "get their man," so they never consider elephants* (italics added).

Behe the biochemist finishes with this smooshing point: "There is an elephant in the roomful of scientists who are trying to explain the development of life. The elephant is labeled 'intelligent design.' "

Recapping the Facts of Life

The whole point of this book, you've no doubt noticed, is that we think evolutionists ignore some *reeeeeally* obvious elephant tracks that indicate a designer behind the natural world.

At the start of *What's With the Mutant in the Microscope?* we said that demonstrating the truth of design—of creation—requires showing how evolutionary theory doesn't accurately explain what we see going on in nature. That point is covered in the first two Facts of Life:

> *Fact of Life #1:* Natural selection is an observable phenomenon that normally maintains rather than changes a species.
>
> *Fact of Life #2:* Exact reproduction of genetic material is necessary for the survival of a species, and

mutations are almost always harmful or deadly.

We also said that confirming creation requires showing how the natural world points to a designer. You saw those truths in the other three Facts of Life:

Fact of Life #3: The intricacy of life—even life in its most basic form, the cell—sure doesn't look like a product of dumb luck. It's evidence of design.

Fact of Life #4: DNA—a living blueprint for how creatures are built—is one screamin' sign of design.

Fact of Life #5: Irreducible complexity makes it impossible for life to have arisen and developed by chance.

We think these are five brain-stompin' signs of design. They're like an elephant doing the cha-cha on your cerebrum. Or the mambo in your medulla oblongata. They're big, brash, and rationally believable.

But if design is so obvious, why doesn't everybody see it?

Knowing Me, Knowing You . . . Uh-huhhh

In chapter one we saw the rules science sets for itself, how science elbows God out of its explanations of life. When scientists start with the assumption that God isn't involved in nature, we noted, they *must* find a natural answer. Studying nature and *not* seeing a designer is a case of *ignoring* clear evidence. But why would evolutionists act like the misguided detectives in Behe's elephant story?

Modern science can teach you a lot of truth. But it can't tell you everything.

Actually, as a *homo sapien* you have three crucial ways to know all that you know. You'll recognize all three methods. Why? Because it takes all three to successfully make toast.

- *Observation* is brains you gain through *senses* or *experience*. Two English guys—philosophers Francis Bacon and John Locke—wrote that what you perceive through sight, hearing, taste, touch, and smell is your main source and final test of knowledge. That theory has been the bent of the Western world ever since. The value of keen observation is why scientists do experiments and why you keep your eyes open when you cross streets.

- *Reason* is knowledge you gain from *logic*. You've probably read about Plato and his world of ideal forms or Descartes' attempt to found his philosophy on "I think, therefore I am." Reason is what "makes sense" to you or what you can determine through systems of proof, like in geometry class. To most of us, reason is knowledge we deduce not out of thin air but from observable facts. Not basing reasoning on observation is how nutcases come to think the Vikings will win a Super Bowl in the next millennium.

- *Revelation* is stuff you know from *God's disclosures of himself.* Moses meeting a burning bush, God preaching through His prophets, and God being born on earth as baby Jesus are all examples of revelation. Revelation teaches you about God, yourself, and your world. It's the knowledge you wouldn't have if God had never said, "Peekaboo! I see you!"

You might be thinking this three-part "epistemology" ("theory of knowledge") looks completely unrelated to the process of making toast.

Trust us. It's not.

What Does Epistemology Have to Do With the Color of Toast?

Making toast is a much more complicated thing than you've ever thunk. It involves, in fact, all three of your key methods of gathering knowledge: observation, reason, and revelation.

Let's set the scene.

You have a toaster. Not one with a fancy heat control picturing various shades of brown, but a simpler one with a knob to set the temperature and a straightforward set of numbers from *1* to *10*.

Still tracking with us?

Through *observation* you've learned that if you set the toaster on *7*, say, you get toast so done it borders on uneatably ugly. A setting of *3*, you've *observed*, yields raw toast. (That's a dangerous thing. Did you know you can get food poisoning from toast that hasn't been heated to an internal temperature of 140 degrees or until all the pink is gone?)

Paying attention? Here's the tricky part.

Reason suggests that putting the toaster on *5* will reward you with toast that's just right. You do an experiment and *observe* that your hypothesis was correct. You could have turned the toaster to *10*. Now, you've probably never turned your toaster all the way up to discover what happens. You're *reasoning* that *10* will char the toast and maybe torch your home. A skeptic could rightly say, "But how do you *know* that *10* doesn't mean 'make it just the way I like it'? You haven't *observed* it."

Disclaimer: In the interests of not incinerating you or your home and getting sued, James and Kevin do *not* recommend driving your toaster faster than federal or local speed limits.

So what does revelation have to do with toast?

Revelation tells you all sorts of facts you might or might not have noticed. It's the sort of stuff that takes eating toast from a bare biological experience to a higher, more human, more spiritual plain:

God gives toast.

Say thanks for toast.

Share toast.

And if you read Kevin's book *Look Who's Toast Now!* you'll discover that *revelation* furthermore says that Satan will be toast at the end of time.

Those are important toast factoids, too. In the grand scheme of things, we'd argue, they're ultimately more important than knowing how to grill perfectly tanned toast. Like Jesus said, "Humans don't live by toast alone" (Matthew 4:4, loosely translated).

Observation Plus Reason Minus Revelation

You probably can guess what science does with our three sources of knowledge. Science is observation and reason gone rigorous. It's observation *plus* reason *minus* revelation.

Picture a toaster factory. There's some serious science going down in the research and development lab. Scientists experiment to see what setting *1* does to a waffle and *8* does to an English muffin. They jot notes on their observations. They reason—they make educated guesses—about watts and wire thicknesses and heat settings. They test and test and test some more to turn out a perfect toaster—one that works for about a year and then dies so you have to buy another one.

We can make some observations about the scientists' observing and reasoning around experimental bread-roasting devices.

First, scientists like system and precision. They aren't the kind of people likely to make the toaster setting *10* a secret code for toast "just the way I like it." Unless they're the guys who inflicted all sorts of rigorous physics experiments on Twinkies. We kid you not (browse to www.twinkiesproject.com).

Second, many scientists see the combination of observation and reason that makes up modern science—*especially* the observation part—as the *only* reliable source of knowledge. They'd note, for example, that it's possible to tan bread and tuck it in your tummy just fine using only observation and reason. They think you don't need revelation to properly do toast or do science, although scientists might allow revealed truth into other parts of their life.

And third, some scientists—*especially* vocal evolutionists—think revelation *really* counts for nothing, because there's nothing real in the universe that you can't see, hear, taste, touch, or smell. "If you can't put it on a scale," as they say, "it doesn't exist." (That's the view called "scientific naturalism" or "materialism" you heard about in chapter one.) But ponder this: If God's revelation is what tells us to share our toast—and they ignore that revelation—it's no wonder that some scientists can cut up human fetuses or create biological weapons or sell poor farmers sterile food seeds without considering right and wrong. Darwinian man is *at best* a monkey shaved. (Or as Martin Luther King Jr. more eloquently described the limitations of science, "We have genuflected before the god of science only to find that it has given us the atomic bomb, producing fears and anxieties that science can never mitigate.")

There's more.

The scientific equation of *observation* plus *reason* minus *revelation* is why people can't see design.

When Science Goes Bad

Science began as an attempt to unravel how God assembled the world, but it became a discipline that unravels as it assembles explanations of the world without God. As we wrap up *What's With the Mutant in the Microscope?* let's look at three basic areas where you'll see creation and evolution clash right before your eyes:

1. Evolutionists—whether guys and gals wearing white lab coats or classmates igniting a bunsen burner next to you at school—likely misunderstand your faith.
2. Evolutionists ignore what revelation teaches about creation.
3. Evolutionists make evolution a religion.
   Let's look at those one by one.

Creation-Evolution Clash #1: Evolutionists Misunderstand Your Faith

You need observation *plus* reason *plus* revelation to get though life—and to get at truth. Whether you're making toast or following God, real life results when you use each of those every minute of every day. Think of what happens when you don't employ all three ways of building your brain:

If you ignore *observation* you "don't deal in reality."

If you ignore *reason* you "lack common sense."

If you ignore *revelation* you're "spiritually dead."

Hardcore scientific naturalists see the Christian faith as a collection of religious myths, one of many collages of myth in the world. *You* need to know that God intends your faith to be rooted in reality—based on all the revelation of God found in the Bible, but reasoned through and tested in experience. Jesus, after all, applauded the honest *reasoning* of Nathanael when Phillip invited him to "come and see" the Savior (John 1:45–51). And Jesus told

His disciples to test His teachings to *observe* if they were true: "If you continue to obey my teaching, you are truly my followers. Then you will know the truth, and the truth will make you free" (John 8:31–32; NCV).

Christian faith didn't just drop from the sky. The Bible *reveals* God. But you have *observable* and *reasonable* evidence for faith, like the facts surrounding the death and resurrection of Jesus, the facts of Israel's history confirmed by archeologists, and the quality and quantity of the manuscripts that communicate the facts of your faith.

For Christians, *observation* and *reason* and *revelation* tightly intertwine. What you learn in the Bible you live out and observe its good effects. You reason about things not directly taught in the Bible. What you learn in life or school through reason or observation you check against the Bible. (Sometimes the Bible clashes with things you think you know. But sometimes you realize you've been reading the Bible wrongly.)

Creation-Evolution Clash #2: Evolutionists Ignore What Revelation Teaches About Creation

Get this one loud and clear: What you've read in chapters one to seven of *What's With the Mutant in the Microscope?* wasn't what evolutionists would think were wacky Bible quotes about creation. We focused on signs of design from nature itself. Evolutionists, though, throw out even this scientifically valid evidence from *observation* and *reason* because it smells like *revelation*. Read your newspaper:

Raising *any* scientific objections to NDMMET or putting forward *any* evidence for design is "sneaking God into the classroom" or "violating the separation of church and state" or "abandoning scientific principle."

We suspect you've learned something about design as you've looked at the cool stuff of creation. The Bible itself says you *should* learn about God through creation. In fact, the Bible says you have to *choose* not to see this "one good reason" to observe God's work in the world:

> The wrath of God is being revealed from heaven against all the godlessness and wickedness of men who suppress the truth by their wickedness, since *what may be known about God is plain to them, because God has made it plain to them. For since the creation of the world God's invisible qualities—his eternal power and divine nature—have been clearly seen, being understood from what has been made,* so that men are without excuse. For although they knew God, they neither glorified him as God nor gave thanks to him, but their thinking became futile and their foolish hearts were darkened. Although they claimed to be wise, they became fools and exchanged the glory of the immortal God for images made to look like mortal man and birds and animals and reptiles (Romans 1:18–23, italics added).

The more you study the interactive and irreducible complexity of creation—cells, DNA, eyeballs, gooky scabs—the more you see God's handiwork and the more you see the truth of the Bible that everything God has made testifies to His great power and wisdom: "The heavens declare the glory of God; the skies proclaim the work of his hands. Day after day they pour forth speech; night after night they display knowledge. There is no speech or language where their voice is not heard" (Psalm 19:1–3).

From God's care for the world (see Matthew 10:29 for how God knows the flight plan of every sparrow on earth) to God's control over creation (spot that power in Jesus' miracles throughout the Gospels) to God's particular interest in human beings (read it in Genesis 1–3), evolutionists rule out a life-altering source of knowledge.

Creation-Evolution Clash #3: Evolutionists Make Evolution a Religion

A few chapters back we said that contemporary science claims to offer "no comment" about God's existence, ruling God outside its realm of knowledge. Just as quickly as evolutionists say they can know nothing about God, though, some create a rigid atheistic belief system.

Exactly how religious are evolutionists in their views? Even when you remember that *scientists* wrote the words below, you can't escape the fact that these are *religious* statements. Stephen Jay Gould, for example, says this:

> Humans [exist] because one odd group of fishes had a particular fin anatomy that could transform into legs for terrestrial creatures; because the earth never froze entirely during an ice age; because a small and tenuous species, arising in Africa a quarter of a million years ago, has managed, so far, to survive by hook and by crook. *We may yearn for a "higher" answer—*

but none exists (italics added).

Cornell University Professor William Provine adds this bit of bad theology:

Modern science directly implies that the world is organized strictly in accordance with mechanistic principles. *There are no purposive principles whatsoever in nature. There are no gods and no designing forces that are rationally detectable* (italics added).

Few evolutionists provide a better example of evolutionary religiosity than Richard Dawkins. You might remember the quote from him at the beginning of the book: "Although atheism might have been *logically* tenable before Darwin, Darwin made it possible to be an intellectually fulfilled atheist." Listen to other assertions he makes in answering the question "Why are people?" Read this one carefully:

Intelligent life on a planet comes of age when it first works out the reason for its own existence. If superior creatures from space ever visit earth, the first question they will ask, in order to assess the level of our civilization, is; "Have they discovered evolution yet?" Living organisms had existed on earth, without every knowing why, for over three thousand million years before the truth finally dawned on them. His name was Charles Darwin. To be fair, others had had inklings of the truth, but it was Darwin who first put together a coherent and tenable account of why we exist. Darwin made it possible for us to give a sensible answer to the curious child whose question heads this chapter. *We no longer have to resort to superstition when faced with the deep problems: Is there a meaning to life? What are we for? What is man?* After posing the last of these questions, the eminent zoologist G.G. Simpson put it thus: "The point I want to make now is that *all attempts to answer that question before 1859 are worthless and that we will be better off if we ignore them completely.*"

Today the theory of evolution is about as much open to doubt as the theory that the earth goes round the sun, but the full implications of Darwin's revolution have yet to be widely realized (italics added).

The real character of Neo-Darwinian Micro-mutational Evolutionary Theory comes out in those first words of Dawkins' book *The Selfish Gene.*

What is truth?

Truth's name is Darwin.

Darwin, Dawkins says, made a sensible answer possible to the question "Why are people?" Not "*What* are people?" (something a scientist is supposed to discuss) but "*Why* are people?" (as in "How'd we get here?" or "What are we here for?" or "Who or what put us here?") A few pages later, he's even more explicit: "Darwin provides a solution, the only feasible one so far suggested, to the deep problem of our existence." He says that, because of Darwin, we know *why* we exist.

Darwin is to evolutionists what Christ is to Christians: truth itself. And don't miss this evolutionary factoid: Until Darwin came along, everyone else had offered only "superstition" and "worthless" answers that "we will be better off if we ignore. . . ."

What the Debate Boils Down To

When you heat something until all the liquid evaporates, you get gunk.

That's the scientific term.

Maybe not.

Well, you get the solid stuff that's all the while been suspended in liquid. When you boil down the conflict between creation and evolution, the dispute comes down to this one point:

Did God do it or not?

Phillip Johnson puts it like this:

> The concept of creation in itself does not imply opposition to evolution, if evolution means only a gradual process by which one kind of living creature changes into something different. A Creator might well have employed such a gradual process as a means of creation. "Evolution" contradicts "creation" only when it is explicitly or tacitly defined as *fully naturalistic evolution*—meaning evolution that is not directed by any purposeful intelligence.

By this point maybe you agree with us that similarities in body structure and genetics don't imply one species—like humans—descended from a radically different species—like apes. Maybe you agree that evolution's mechanism of natural selection plus mutations doesn't work. But the atheism part—the "fully naturalistic evolution," the God-didn't-have-anything-to-do-with-designing-life-on-this-planet part—is where we hope you really choke.

The Choice Is Yours

In evolutionary thinking, dumb luck is the ultimate decision-maker. There's no room for the Christian God. Evolutionary theory asks that you accept a tightly wrapped package. It includes facts we can all accept, like the jaw-dropping diversity of life. But it's wrapped up with nasty stuff like descent, evolution—and ultimately atheism.

Remember the rat and the snake in chapter two?

You're the snake.

NDMMET is the rat.

You're supposed to swallow it whole.

It's your choice: Did every living thing come to exist on its own through random forces—or does it take a Creator to explain what you see?

If you have proof that what you see in the world is the product of dumb luck, that's all you need to dispense with a designer.

On the other hand, if there's design, there's an intelligent Designer.

A Worldmaker.

A Creator of you, me, and the natural world we see.

A *Who* who made you.

That's the most fundamental claim of creationism.

It's really what the dispute boils down to.

We hope you acknowledge there's a God who made you.

He gives you toast.

Give thanks.

Remember to share.

WHAT'S WITH THE MUTANT IN THE MICROSCOPE?

Study Questions

1. List and explain the five Facts of Life in *What's With the Mutant in the Microscope?*

2. How do observation, reason, and revelation work in real life? What is the basis of the arguments in chapters one to seven in *Mutant*? Why would these arguments be rejected by hard-core scientists? Why are they important to debunking evolutionary theory?

3. What's an elephant got to do with evolution? What's toast got to do with epistemology? Is your Christian faith based purely on revelation?

4. What three things happen when science goes bad?

5. After reading *What's With the Mutant in the Microscope?* what do you think about evolution?

Sources and Resources for More Reading

Behe, Michael J. *Darwin's Black Box*. New York: Free Press, 1996.

Bohinski, Robert C. *Modern Concepts in Biochemistry*. Boston: Allyn and Bacon, Inc., 1987.

Burns, George W. *The Science of Genetics: An Introduction to Heredity*. New York: Macmillan Publishing Co., 1980.

Calladine, C. R., and Drew, Horace R. *Understanding DNA: The Molecule and How It Works*. San Diego: Academic Press, Inc., 1997.

Curtis, Helena. *Biology*. New York: Worth Publishers, Inc., 1979.

Dawkins, Richard. *The Blind Watchmaker*. New York: W. W. Norton & Company, 1986.

———, *The Selfish Gene*. New York: Oxford University Press, 1976.

Dembski, William A., ed., *Mere Creation: Science, Faith & Intelligent Design*. Downers Grove, Ill.: InterVarsity Press, 1998.

Denton, Michael. *Evolution: A Theory in Crisis*. Bethesda, Md.: Adler & Adler, 1986.

Frank-Kamenetski, Maxim D. *Unraveling DNA: The Most Important Molecule of Life*. Reading, Mass.: Addison-Wesley, 1997.

Ferris, Timothy. *The Whole Shebang: A State-of-the-Universe Report*. New York: Touchstone, 1997.

Goodsell, David S. *The Machinery of Life.* New York: Copernicus, 1998.

———, *Our Molecular Nature.* New York: Copernicus, 1996.

Gould, Stephen J. *Wonderful Life.* New York: W. W. Norton & Company, 1989.

Guyton, Arthur C., M.D. *Human Physiology and Mechanisms of Disease.* Philadelphia: W. B. Saunders Company, 1982.

Hayward, Alan. *Creation and Evolution.* Minneapolis: Bethany House Publishers, 1995.

Johnson, Phillip E. *Darwin on Trial.* Downers Grove, Ill.: InterVarsity Press, 1991.

———, *Defeating Darwinism by Opening Minds.* Downers Grove, Ill.: InterVarsity Press, 1997.

Moreland, J. P., ed., *The Creation Hypothesis: Scientific Evidence for an Intelligent Designer.* Downers Grove, Ill.: InterVarsity Press, 1994.

Pollack, Robert. *Signs of Life.* New York: Houghton Mifflin Company, 1994.

Schwartz, Jeffrey H. *Sudden Origins.* New York: John Wiley and Sons, 1999.

Thaxton, Charles; Bradley, Walter, and Olsen, Roger. *The Mystery of Life's Origin: Reassessing Current Theories.* New York: Philosophical Library, 1984.

Tortora, Gerard J., and Anagnostakos, Nicholas P. *Principles of Anatomy and Physiology.* New York: Harper & Row, Publishers, 1981.

Wilcox, Frank H. *DNA: The Thread of Life.* Minneapolis: Lerner Publications Company, 1988.